Cambridge Elements

Elements in the Gothic
edited by
Dale Townshend
Manchester Metropolitan University
Angela Wright
University of Sheffield

GOTHIC POLAND AND BRITISH FICTION, C. 1790–1830

Jakub Lipski
Kazimierz Wielki University

Shaftesbury Road, Cambridge CB2 8EA, United Kingdom

One Liberty Plaza, 20th Floor, New York, NY 10006, USA

477 Williamstown Road, Port Melbourne, VIC 3207, Australia

314–321, 3rd Floor, Plot 3, Splendor Forum, Jasola District Centre, New Delhi – 110025, India

103 Penang Road, #05–06/07, Visioncrest Commercial, Singapore 238467

Cambridge University Press is part of Cambridge University Press & Assessment, a department of the University of Cambridge.

We share the University's mission to contribute to society through the pursuit of education, learning and research at the highest international levels of excellence.

www.cambridge.org
Information on this title: www.cambridge.org/9781009548212

DOI: 10.1017/9781009435048

© Jakub Lipski 2025

This publication is in copyright. Subject to statutory exception and to the provisions of relevant collective licensing agreements, no reproduction of any part may take place without the written permission of Cambridge University Press & Assessment.

When citing this work, please include a reference to the DOI 10.1017/9781009435048

First published 2025

A catalogue record for this publication is available from the British Library

ISBN 978-1-009-54821-2 Hardback
ISBN 978-1-009-43507-9 Paperback
ISSN 2634-8721 (online)
ISSN 2634-8713 (print)

Cambridge University Press & Assessment has no responsibility for the persistence or accuracy of URLs for external or third-party internet websites referred to in this publication and does not guarantee that any content on such websites is, or will remain, accurate or appropriate.

For EU product safety concerns, contact us at Calle de José Abascal, 56, 1°, 28003 Madrid, Spain, or email eugpsr@cambridge.org

Gothic Poland and British Fiction, c. 1790–1830

Elements in the Gothic

DOI: 10.1017/9781009435048
First published online: December 2025

Jakub Lipski
Kazimierz Wielki University
Author for correspondence: Jakub Lipski, j.lipski@ukw.edu.pl

Abstract: This Element demonstrates how Poland became a gothic setting in British fiction between the 1790s and the 1830s as a result of public interest in the partitions of Poland (1772–95) and their aftermath. It first discusses the ways Minerva gothics capitalised on the appeal of the Polish cause and showcases salient patterns for the 'gothicisation' of Poland. This is followed by two focused readings of texts – Jane Porter's *Thaddeus of Warsaw* (1803) and Catherine Gore's *Polish Tales* (1833) – that build on this tradition and further explore the potential of female gothic frameworks and the gothic's long-standing investment in war and revolution to generalise and allegorise the political turmoil in Poland. This Element argues that the idea of Gothic Poland in British fiction was negotiated between the particular and the universal, the familiar and the unknown, the need for historical and factual accuracy and the prevalent patterns of gothic obfuscation.

Keywords: Gothic, Minerva Press, Poland in British fiction, Continental spaces in the British gothic, Gothic setting

© Jakub Lipski 2025

ISBNs: 9781009548212 (HB), 9781009435079 (PB), 9781009435048 (OC)
ISSNs: 2634-8721 (online), 2634-8713 (print)

Contents

	Introduction	1
1	Poland in Minerva Gothics	10
2	Jane Porter's *Thaddeus of Warsaw* (1803): Poland and the Gothic Underplots	30
3	Catherine Gore's *Polish Tales* (1833): Complicating Poland's Victimhood	43
	Conclusion	62
	Bibliography	65

Gothic Poland and British Fiction, c. 1790–1830 1

Introduction

The story of late eighteenth-century Poland is a gothic one. It is a story of abuse, intrigue over land and property, persecuted innocence, and monstrous dismemberment. It is also a story of the country's 'ancient magnificence' gradually falling into ruin; a transition from one of Europe's most powerful states in the late seventeenth century – the Polish-Lithuanian Commonwealth – into a helpless bystander on the political stage. Finally, it is also a story that reverses gendered powerplay, featuring a villainous female tyrant, Empress Catherine II, typically seen as endowed with conventionally masculine features, and her former plaything and then unsuccessful rebel Stanisław August Poniatowski, the last king of Poland, often characterised as effeminate and deprived of agency.[1] Poniatowski in chains is used as a personification of Poland in Isaac Cruikshank's graphic satire of 1796, 'The moment of reflection, or, A tale for future times!!', which pictures a grotesquely monstrous Catherine (uncovering her devilish hoof) as she nears her death, haunted by the havoc she has wrought in Poland (Figure 1). The allegorical function is also performed by the Madonna-like mother with child, in the top-left corner, brutally massacred by the approaching soldiers.

The events leading from Stanisław August's ascension to the throne in 1764, orchestrated by Catherine, to the third partition of Poland in 1795 attracted substantial public attention in Western Europe, including Great Britain. The king's struggles with the opposition (most notably with the Bar Confederacy, who carried out the unsuccessful assassination plot of 1771), his enlightened attempts at reforming the state and liberating it from Russian supervision (such as the declaration of the Constitution of 3 May 1791), and especially the three partitions themselves: the first in 1772, the second in 1793, and the third, leading to what was labelled the 'dismemberment' of the country, were all sensational and politically relevant material for news coverage, especially when seen against the broader panorama of European and transatlantic politics throughout the final decades of the eighteenth century: the ongoing wars, revolutions, and the issues of slavery and abolition.[2] The Polish-Russian wars of 1792 and 1794 were seen as heroic eruptions of a dying state, which added a tinge of Romantic flair to the myth as well as underlining its horrific aspects – most tangibly exemplified by the infamous massacre of Praga, a district of Warsaw, poignantly represented by Isaac Cruikshank in 'Royal Recreation' (Figure 2), which depicts General Alexander

---

[1] When referring to the king as a historical figure, I retain the original Polish spelling Stanisław. When discussing literary characters modelled on the king, I follow the spellings used by respective authors.

[2] For an accessible historical overview of these events, their aftermath, and continuing cultural and political currency in Poland, see Norman Davies, *Heart of Europe: The Past in Poland's Present* (Oxford: Oxford University Press, 2001), pp. 138–48; 269–77.

Figure 1 Isaac Cruikshank, 'The moment of reflection, or, A tale for future times!!', 1796, Courtesy of the Lewis Walpole Library.

Figure 2 Isaac Cruikshank, Royal Recreation, 1795, Yale Center for British Art, Paul Mellon Collection

Suvorov fulfilling Catherine's 'Tender Affectionate & Maternal Commission to those Deluded People of Poland' and presenting the empress with 'Picklings of Ten Thousand Heads tenderly detached from their deluded bodies', as can be read in the general's speech balloon.

The 1794 uprising, led by General Tadeusz Kościuszko, a hero of the American War of Independence, and the consequent fall of Poland were followed by the so-called 'Kościuszko craze' at the turn of the eighteenth century, which also reached Britain upon the exiled war hero's sojourn in London and Bristol in 1796–7. The collective memory of the events of the 1790s continued throughout the ensuing years and decades, along with the continually pronounced presence of 'the Polish cause' during the Napoleonic wars and their aftermath, which culminated in the establishment of Congress Poland in 1815, only to gather momentum again during and after the November Uprising of 1830–1, and the subsequent emigration of Polish exiles to France and Britain.

Between the 1790s and the 1830s the Polish cause was a regular topic of news coverage, non-fiction publications, travel writing, and creative forms of literature, including poetry and prose fiction. So far, critical attention has primarily been given to traces of this presence in non-fiction and, especially, in poetry. John Howes Gleason, Wojciech Lipoński, Wojciech Jasiakiewicz, and also Miłosz K. Cybowski have undertaken considerable work in mapping the political connections between Poland and Britain in the period as reflected in contemporary non-fiction, press items, and parliamentary debates.[3] Poetic expressions of sympathy towards Poland, most memorably captured in George Galloway's collection *Poems. The Tears of Poland* (1795) and Thomas Campbell's *Pleasures of Hope* (1799), as well as the importance of 'the Kościuszko craze' for mainstream Romantic poets, such as Samuel Taylor Coleridge, John Keats, Percy Bysshe Shelley, and Leigh Hunt, who all wrote lyrical pieces dedicated to Kościuszko, have been well documented and will continue to generate discussion.[4] The less-trodden area is prose fiction, with Jane Porter's *Thaddeus of Warsaw* being the

---

[3] John Howes Gleason, *The Genesis of Russophobia in Great Britain: A Study of the Interaction of Policy and Opinion* (Cambridge, MA: Harvard University Press, 1950), pp. 107–34; Wojciech Lipoński, *Polska a Brytania 1801–1830: Próby politycznego i cywilizacyjnego dźwignięcia kraju w oparciu o Wielką Brytanię* (Poznań: Wydawnictwo Naukowe Uniwersytetu im. Adama Mickiewicza w Poznaniu, 1978); Wojciech Jasiakiewicz, *Brytyjska opinia publiczna wobec powstania listopadowego w okresie 1830–1834* (Toruń: Wydawnictwo Uniwersytetu Mikołaja Kopernika, 1997); Milosz K. Cybowski, 'The Polish Questions in British Politics and Beyond, 1830–1847' (PhD diss., University of Southampton, 2016).

[4] See, among others, Francis E. Zapatka, 'Kościuszko among the English Romantics', *The Polish Review* 30:3 (1985): 239–53; Thomas McLean, *The Other East and Nineteenth-Century British Literature: Imagining Poland and the Russian Empire* (Basingstoke: Palgrave Macmillan, 2012), pp. 1–65; Sarah Zimmerman, 'Thomas Campbell, Scholar-Poet', in *The Romantic Literary Lecture in Britain* (Oxford: Oxford University Press, 2019), pp. 91–117.

only Poland-centred narrative of the period that has been critically read and acknowledged, with various insights coming from the work of Thomas McLean, Devoney Looser, Fiona Price, Maciej Laskowski, and Zofia Gołębiowska.[5] Overlooking the ways in which fiction addresses the Polish cause in the period is arguably one further, if belated, expression of traditional canonisation, grounded in Wordsworthian categories of genius, which prioritised lyrical poetry and discarded fictional 'trash'. Piotr J. Drozdowski's survey articles on 'Echoes of the Polish Revolution in Late Eighteenth and Early Nineteenth Century English Literature' focus almost exclusively on poetry, with only a brief acknowledgement of some coverage of these issues in the press.[6] In the more recent collection *Polish Culture in Britain: Literature and History, 1772 to the Present*, the chapters covering the period 1790–1830 comment on the relevant fiction merely by listing several titles in a single sentence, though the approach here is mainly historiographic and as such privileges non-fiction.[7]

In a similar manner, Poland has been consistently absent from critical discussions of how British gothic fiction imaginatively mapped Europe in the period in question. These discussions have so far prioritised, and understandably so, the central role of France and the French Revolution for the development of the early gothic, and the prevalence of Mediterranean settings as the repository of popular imagery, not least due to the documented influence of canonical examples of the genre, including Ann Radcliffe's and Matthew Gregory Lewis's fiction, which remained a point of reference for subsequent authors, and whose depictions of France, Italy, and Spain would become a model for a creative gothicisation of Continental spaces.[8] At the same time, attention has been paid to likely sources

---

[5] See, for example, Zofia Gołębiowska, 'Jane Porter – angielska admiratorka Tadeusza Kościuszki', *Annales Universitatis Mariae Curie-Skłodowska* 56 (2001): 7–15; McLean, *The Other East*, pp. 66–87; Devoney Looser, 'The Great Man and Women's Historical Fiction: Jane Porter and Sir Sidney Smith', *Women's Writing* 19:3 (2012): 293–314; Maciej Laskowski, 'Jane Porter's *Thaddeus of Warsaw* as Evidence of Polish-British Relationships' (PhD diss., Adam Mickiewicz University, 2012); Fiona Price, *Reinventing Liberty: Nation, Commerce and the Historical Novel from Walpole to Scott* (Edinburgh: Edinburgh University Press, 2016).

[6] Piotr J. Drozdowski, 'Echoes of the Polish Revolution in Late Eighteenth and Early Nineteenth Century English Literature (A Selection of Works and Voices: Part One)', *The Polish Review* 38:1 (1993): 3–24; Piotr J. Drozdowski, 'Echoes of the Polish Revolution in Late Eighteenth and Early Nineteenth Century English Literature (A Selection of Works and Voices: Part Two)', *The Polish Review* 38:2 (1993): 131–48.

[7] Adam Zamoyski, 'From the Moon to Kennington Common: British Perceptions of the Poland and the Poles 1750–1850'; Milosz K. Cybowski, 'Brave and Patriotic Poles: British Politics and Polish Independence, 1830–1847', in Maggie Ann Bowers and Ben Dew (eds), *Polish Culture in Britain: Literature and History, 1772 to the Present* (Cham: Palgrave Macmillan, 2023), pp. 17–61.

[8] See, among others, 'Italy and the Gothic', special issue of *Gothic Studies* 8:1 (2006); Angela Wright, *Britain, France and the Gothic, 1764–1820: The Import of Terror* (Cambridge: Cambridge University Press, 2013); Evan Gottlieb, 'No Place Like Home: From Local to Global (and Back Again) in the Gothic Novel', in Evan Gottlieb and Juliet Sheilds (eds), *Representing Place in British Literature and Culture: From Local to Global, 1660–1830* (Farnham: Ashgate,

of inspiration, such as the German *Schauerroman*, which resulted in the popularity of Germany as the setting for narratives written in this vein, several of which were included in the famous list of 'horrid' novels recommended by Isabella Thorpe in Jane Austen's *Northanger Abbey* (1818).[9] The map of gothic Europe, as reconstructed through critical readings of British fiction of the period, is thus incomplete and affected by what has typically been considered canonical or more popular, leaving blanks that merit scholarly focus.[10]

In an attempt to redress these critical tendencies, this Element demonstrates how British interest in the politically troubled situation in Poland between the 1790s and the 1830s translated into Poland being used as a setting in contemporaneous British prose fiction. Since, as suggested earlier, the story of what happened in Poland in this period is inherently gothic, my aim here is to show how fiction writers responded to these events by deploying appropriate gothic conventions. As my material will exemplify, the meanings behind the eponymous 'gothic setting' are not uniform. Poland offered conventional spaces that were explored in gothic fiction set elsewhere, such as ruins, mountains, dark forests, and feudal edifices. The relevant fiction was also enriched by more specific spatial representations of concrete loci that were endowed with what might be termed 'gothic appeal', including labyrinthine salt mines, ancient forests, or the Polish frontier, which separated the western world from the 'barbarians' of the east. At the same time, this material engaged with the conceptual potential of Gothic Poland, oscillating between mutually exclusive – one should think – categories of a 'dark' and 'magnificent' past, villainy and victimhood, as well as barbarism and enlightened modernism. The suspension of binaries would be one gothic technique deployed repeatedly across the corpus; other conventions included temporal and geographical obfuscation, along the lines of the Burkean aesthetic of obscurity, and spatial and historical confusion (by means of shrinking, blending, mixing fact with fiction) resulting from a creative bricolage of what was known and what, enticingly, remained unknown.[11]

2013), pp. 85–101; Angela Wright, 'Spain in Gothic Fiction', in Diego Saglia and Ian Haywood (eds), *Spain in British Romanticism, 1800–1840* (Cham: Palgrave Macmillan, 2018), pp. 177–93.

[9] See, for example, Andrew Cusack and Barry Murnane (eds), *Popular Revenants: The German Gothic and Its International Reception, 1800–2000* (Rochester: Camden House, 2012).

[10] A recent collection of essays on depictions of Europe in the gothic goes significantly beyond the early gothic and offers insight into a greater variety of spaces depicted, yet Poland remains absent from this discussion. See Michael Newton and Evert Jan van Leeuwen (eds), *Haunted Europe: Continental Connections in English-Language Gothic Writing, Film and New Media* (London and New York: Routledge, 2020).

[11] As Edmund Burke famously put it, 'It is one thing to make an idea clear, and another to make it *affecting* to the imagination'. Edmund Burke, *A Philosophical Enquiry into the Origin of our Ideas of the Sublime and Beautiful*, edited by Adam Phillips (Oxford: Oxford University Press, 1998), p. 55.

Proceeding from the absorption of Poland into the gothic universe of William Lane and A. K. Newman's Minerva Press, which dominated the gothic publishing market at the turn of the eighteenth century (Section 1), to the uses of the gothic mode in Jane Porter's 1803 *Thaddeus of Warsaw* (Section 2), and Catherine Gore's 1833 *Polish Tales* (Section 3), I will demonstrate both how the gothic tradition was enriched by specifically Polish geographies – at times represented with factual accuracy, at times intentionally deformed – and how well-established gothic conventions, ranging from spatial representation to plot design, helped to adjust the new content to readerly expectations and were used to make sense of Poland's past and present. Through focused readings of Porter's and Gore's narratives, I will underline how these authors were able to raise wider concerns about war, revolution, class, enslavement, and the position of women through generalising and allegorising the Poland-centred subject matter.

This Element is concerned with how Poland was represented in British fiction, and, indeed, the specific realities of the British response to what was happening in Poland between 1771 and 1830 legitimise such a focused perspective. At the same time, by way of acknowledging the immediate literary context, it must be borne in mind that the Polish cause was not awarded exclusive attention in *British* poetry, fiction, and non-fiction. While studying literary responses to the partitions of Poland in the German or French languages is beyond the scope of the present study, it is worth pointing out that the narratives examined in detail in the subsequent sections of this Element sat alongside comparable ventures that became part of the British literary network through translation. For example, the English edition of *The Life and Adventures of the Chevalier de Faublas* (1793) was promoted to the English reader 'as including a variety of anecdotes relative to the present King of Poland' – a subtitle that was not used in the original French volumes.[12] Readers of Minerva gothics, in turn, could relate what they read in original productions to the narratives adopted from other languages, such as Charles-Antoine Pigault-Lebrun's *The Polanders* (1805) or Heinrich Zschokke's *The Polish Chieftain* (1806), referring to the times of Stefan Batory, as the original German title makes clear: *Stephan Bathori, König von Polen* (1796).[13] The popular French narrative of an exiled Polish woman, *Pauliska, ou la perversité moderne* (1798), was not translated into English in the period, but

---

[12] Jean-Baptiste Louvet de Couvray, *The Life and Adventures of the Chevalier de Faublas: Including a Variety of Anecdotes Relative to the Present King of Poland*, 4 vols (London: R. Faudler, 1793).

[13] Charles-Antoine Pigault-Lebrun, *The Polanders; The Lying Family; and The Life of My Uncle, with His Portfolio* (London: Minerva, 1805); Heinrich Zschokke, *The Polish Chieftain* (London: Minerva, 1806).

it was promoted by the London-based imprint of J. De Boffe as exceeding the terrifying *Justine* (1791) by the Marquis de Sade.[14] Its shadowy presence in Britain is further suggested by an 1829 historical play staged at Covent Garden Theatre, *The Battle of Pultawa: The King and the Czar*, which features a character called Pauliska, even if its historical context is different from that of the French novel. A gothic bluebook titled *Lodoiska; or, The Tartar Robber* (1811) was based, in turn, on a French comic opera by Luigi Cherubini that premiered on 18 July 1791 at the Théâtre Feydeau in Paris.[15] A sustained reading of these and similar narratives in their original languages and contexts, also taking into account the actual Polish presence in these countries in the period in question (especially in France), is a subject worth pursuing elsewhere.

A similar point should be made about narratives in the period that fashion themselves as Russian tales, despite the fact that – strictly speaking – a large part of dismembered Poland was absorbed by Catherine II's empire and was, in geopolitical terms, part of Russia. In terms of spatial representation, however, narratives such as Mary Charlton's *Phedora; or, the Forest of Minski* (1798), August Lafontaine's *Dolgorucki and Menzikof. A Russian Tale* (English version published in 1805), or the anonymous *Demetrius, a Russian Romance* (1813) constitute a related but separate corpus of material.[16] Even though the proximity of Poland is mapped and acknowledged in these narratives, this Element addresses the spatial imagery revolving around the traditionally Polish axis, from the Cracow region, to Warsaw, and finally to Vilnius in present-day Lithuania. As will be seen, Gothic Poland was not consistently mapped as part of the East, but was instead drawn closer to the already established imagery of the Mediterranean South.

The other type of material that falls beyond my scope, but which is nevertheless worth acknowledging, includes narratives that introduce the Polish theme, most probably due to heightened interest in the country in the period in question, but which do not conceptualise Poland as a gothic setting. The eponymous protagonist of Margaret Minifie's *The Count de Poland* (1780) shares a melancholic and mysterious disposition with the hero of Jane Porter's *Thaddeus of Warsaw*, but Minifie's epistolary narrative is set in London, and there is little background knowledge of the count that readers could link to specific events in Poland.[17] Partly factual, partly fictional *Memoirs of the Celebrated Dwarf, Joseph Boruwlaski* (translated from the French, 1788, 2nd.

---

[14] M. Peltier, *Paris, Pendant L'Année 1798* (Londres: Deboffe, Dulau, Boosey, 1798), p. 194.

[15] *Lodoiska; or, The Tartar Robber: An Historic Tale* (London: J. Roe & Ann Lemoine, 1811).

[16] Mary Charlton, *Phedora; or, the Forest of Minski*, 4 vols (London: Minerva, 1798); August Heinrich Julius Lafontaine, *Dolgorucki and Menzikof. A Russian Tale*, 2 vols (London: Minerva, 1805); *Demetrius, a Russian Romance*, 2 vols (London: Longman, 1813).

[17] Margaret Minifie, *The Count de Poland*, 4 vols (London: J. Dodsley, 1780).

ed. 1792) and *The Memoirs and Travels of Mauritius August Count de Benyowsky* (first published in English and promoted as translated from the original Polish manuscript in 1790) both echo political specificities – Boruwlaski spent years at Stanisław August's court, while Beniowski was a member of the anti-royal Bar Confederacy – but the setting in these adventurous narratives is, in a sense, the whole globe, rather than specifically Poland.[18] Mrs Murray's novel *Henry Count de Kolinski* (1810), which reveals some affinities with Beniowski's memoir, tells the story of an unhappy lover exiled to Siberia who eventually manages to secure a happy life for himself in America and Britain, having escaped from the Russian desert using an air balloon he constructed with the assistance of a Chinese tradesman.[19] The exile into Russia links the narrative to specific political realities, but the scope of Kolinski's adventures, like Beniowski's, brings to mind Rudolf Raspe's preposterous *Baron Munchausen* (1785), which at one point also takes the reader to Poland.

In Raspe's narrative Poland is a country of cold and snow: forced to spend the night outdoors, the baron ties his horse to what he takes to be a tree. The snow melts away overnight, and upon waking, the baron sees his horse tied to a cross on top of a church steeple, which he mistakenly thought was a tree when being raised by the grotesquely thick layer of snow.[20] Thomas Rowlandson's depiction of the scene (Figure 3) does not even note that the event takes place in Poland, highlighting instead the Baron's skills at shooting (he targets the bridle that ties the horse), which suggests that the specific spatial contexts of Munchausen's antics are a mere background to the main character's escapades and achievements.

A similar, character-oriented perspective – however different the actual narratives are – is adopted in one of the better-known fictions that address the Polish revolutions, here the 1830 uprising: Claire Clairmont and Mary Shelley's short story 'The Pole' (1832). A Radcliffean tale of intrigue and treachery, it features the titular Ladislaus, who is given a memorable sketch that suggests the influence of Porter's *Thaddeus* and the still prevalent fascination with Kościuszko:

> In stature he was tall, and his form was moulded in such perfect proportions, that it presented a rare combination of youthful lightness and manly strength. His countenance, had you taken from it its deep thoughtfulness and its expression of calm intrepid bravery, might have belonged to the most lovely

---

[18] Joseph Boruwlaski, *Memoires du Célèbre Nain Joseph Boruwlaski; Memoirs of the Celebrated Dwarf, Joseph Boruwlaski* (Londres/London, 1788); Mauritius August Count de Benyowsky; *The Memoirs and Travels of Mauritius August Count de Benyowsky*, 2 vols (London: G. G. J. and J. Robinson, 1790).

[19] Mrs. Murray, *Henry Count de Kolinski: A Polish Tale* (London: James Cawthorn, 1810).

[20] Rudolph Erich Raspe, *Gulliver Revived; or the Singular Travels, Campaigns, Voyages, and Adventures of Baron Munikhouson, Commonly Called Munchausen*, 3rd ed. (Oxford: G. Kearsley, 1786), pp. 6–9.

Figure 3 Thomas Rowlandson, The Baron Proves Himself a Good Shot, 1809, the Metropolitan Museum of Art, The Elisha Whittelsey Collection, The Elisha Whittelsey Fund, 1959

woman, so transparently blooming was his complexion, so regular his features, so blond and luxuriant his hair.[21]

A curious mix of effeminacy and manliness, with a tinge of melancholy, was a stock trope in representing exiled Poles modelled on Kościuszko and Stanisław August. While the title might suggest otherwise, 'The Pole' does not use Poland as a setting; the story takes place in Italy, but even there Ladislaus is victim to a persecution orchestrated by a Russian aristocrat.

Sustained interest in the country from the 1790s onwards brought the English reader closer to the actual Polish realities, which ran parallel with real-life contact with Polish immigrants in Britain. William Coxe's 1784 *Travels into Poland, Russia, Sweden, and Denmark* ran into six editions in 1785, 1787, 1790, 1791, 1792. For a piece of travel writing, this was an outstanding afterlife. Coxe's travelogue was not the only source of knowledge for fiction writers, but it was a very significant one, at times openly acknowledged, as we shall see.[22] Coxe's narrative contains extensive historiographic passages, some of which were adopted by Stephen Jones in *The History of Poland* of 1795; a Dublin publication of the same year suggests that it was widely read.[23] Other factual

---

[21] Mary Shelley [and Claire Clairmont], 'The Pole', in Mary Wollstonecraft Shelley, *Tales and Stories* (London: William Paterson, 1891), pp. 274–310 (pp. 274–5).

[22] William Coxe, *Travels into Poland, Russia, Sweden, and Denmark*, 2 vols (London: T. Cadell, 1784).

[23] Stephen Jones, *History of Poland* (London: Vernor and Hood, 1795).

accounts of the 1790s Poland included *Memorial on the Present State of Poland* (1791), *An Authentic Narrative of Facts Relative to the Late Dismemberment of Poland* (1794), and John Adams's *A View of Universal History . . . Including an Account of the Celebrated Revolutions in France, Poland, Sweden, Geneva* (1795);[24] these and similar publications were complemented by the extensive coverage the Polish question was receiving in the contemporary press. This surge of interest in the 1790s revolution was repeated, with even more force, in the context of the 1830 uprising.[25]

At the same time, images of a fantasy-like Poland were continuously present in the British imagination. When Edmund Burke realised that the best sympathetic sentiments towards the country's unjust struggles would not translate into actual political activism in Britain, given unresolvable differences in international interests and allegiances, he famously remarked during a parliamentary debate on 17 June 1793: 'with respect to us, Poland might be, in fact, considered as a country in the moon'.[26] This metaphor, whether intentionally or not, situates Poland in the context of the spatial conventions of eighteenth-century imaginary voyages, which *Baron Munchausen* exemplifies. As this Element will show, while the representations of Gothic Poland in fiction between the 1790s and the 1830s demonstrate, with varying degrees, a drive towards factual saturation, the fantastic charm of a 'country in the moon' is never entirely lost.

1 Poland in Minerva Gothics

The partitions of Poland coincided with the rise of the Minerva Press as the leading publishing house for popular fiction. The imprint established by William Lane in the 1780s was, from the very beginning, responsive to prevalent political topics,[27] but it was with its rebranding as 'Minerva' in 1790, which was shortly after proudly displayed on title pages in recognisable gothic font, that the press's specialism became gothic fiction. This fiction was typically dismissed, especially when juxtaposed with the admired achievements of Ann Radcliffe and Matthew Gregory Lewis, on whose variants of the gothic much of Minerva fiction was modelled, alongside imports from France and Germany.

---

[24] *Memorial on the Present State of Poland* (London: J. Debrett, 1791); *An Authentic Narrative of Facts Relative to the Late Dismemberment of Poland* (London: J. Owen, 1794); John Adams, *A View of Universal History . . . Including an Account of the Celebrated Revolutions in France, Poland, Sweden, Geneva* (London: G. Kearsley, 1795).

[25] See Gleason, *The Genesis of Russophobia in Great Britain*, pp. 107–34; Jasiakiewicz, *Brytyjska opinia publiczna wobec powstania listopadowego w okresie 1830–1834*.

[26] Edmund Burke, *The Speeches of the Right Honourable Edmund Burke in the House of Commons and in Westminster Hall*, 4 vols (London: Longman, Hurst, Rees, Orme and Brown, 1816), vol. 4, p. 148.

[27] Joe Lines, 'William Lane, the Ramble Novel and the Genres of Romantic Irish Fiction', *Romantic Textualities: Literature and Print Culture, 1780–1840* 23 (2020): 21–38.

The aesthetic of 'secondary' writing and stylistic excess, structural parallelisms and repetitions, spatial and temporal obfuscation and ambiguity were typically read as indicators of hasty writing, authors' ignorance, and the press's mechanistic approach to literary production as well as its unrestrained pursuit of commercial gain.[28]

In contrast, contemporary – still burgeoning – research into Minerva-published fictions has convincingly established the significance of this tradition.[29] Far from being thoughtlessly derivative, poor-quality narratives, these texts provide unique insight into how the post-Radcliffean and post-Lewisite gothic developed, help us to reconsider the conventional prioritisation of lyrical poetry in historical approaches to Romantic literature, and are testimony to the mechanics of literary production in the period. The appearance of Poland in Minerva gothic demonstrates the responsiveness of the Minerva universe to the topical issues of the time. Authors associated with this publishing house undertook the Polish cause with an immediacy that was generally typical of how they responded to whatever happened and was published. The fast turnaround time, with writers being able to deliver complete manuscripts in a matter of weeks, translated into Minerva's important role as an instantaneous mirror of public interest. With respect to the common criticism of the press's complete dependence on literary recycling – which facilitated the authors' fast-paced writing – Franz Potter suggests that this allowed 'the Gothic tradition to continue to be viewed in the larger context of evolving discourses'.[30] While Potter addresses the genre's mutability in the light of changing fashions, and especially the popularity of historical romances after the publication of Walter Scott's *Waverley* in 1814, Minerva's interconnectedness with 'evolving discourses' can also be seen in how it interacted with issues on the socio-political front. Indeed, as Mark Canuel succinctly puts it with reference to religious affairs, 'the Parliamentary debates of the late eighteenth and early nineteenth centuries mobilized the plots and images of the Gothic novel'.[31]

---

[28] Hannah Doherty Hudson, *Romantic Fiction and Literary Excess in the Minerva Press Era* (Cambridge: Cambridge University Press, 2023), pp. 1–8.

[29] Franz J. Potter, *The History of Gothic Publishing, 1800–1835: Exhuming the Trade* (Basingstoke: Palgrave Macmillan, 2005); Elizabeth A. Neiman, *Minerva's Gothics: The Politics and Poetics of Romantic Exchange, 1780–1820* (Cardiff: University of Wales Press, 2019); Elizabeth Neiman and Christina Morin (eds), 'The Minerva Press and the Literary Marketplace', a special issue of *Romantic Textualities: Literature and Print Culture, 1780–1840* 23 (2020); Yael Shapira, 'The Gothic Novel Beyond Radcliffe and Lewis', in Angela Wright and Dale Townshend (eds), *The Cambridge History of the Gothic. Volume I: Gothic in the Long Eighteenth Century* (Cambridge: Cambridge University Press, 2020), pp. 323–44; Hudson, *Romantic Fiction and Literary Excess in the Minerva Press Era*.

[30] Potter, *The History of Gothic Publishing*, p. 8.

[31] Mark Canuel, *Religion, Toleration and British Writing, 1790–1830* (Cambridge: Cambridge University Press, 2002), p. 55.

Minerva authors did not make Poland a setting comparable, in its coverage, to Germany or Southern European countries, but the Poland-set fictions provide invaluable insight into how the machinery of Minerva gothic, endowed with an uncanny agency of its own, absorbed Poland into its universe: how the country both enriched that universe with its own specificities and was adjusted to align with what Minerva readers expected as far as landscape and architectural descriptions were concerned. The political turmoil in the country, and its inherently gothic allure, in turn, would have suggested to Minerva authors several plot patterns and motifs that, while not new, would have acquired specific, politically relevant meanings when read against the background of Poland's dismemberment: anti-royal conspiracies, stories of dispossession, and allusions and references to historical figures would have brought the familiar Minerva narratives closer to what was happening in Poland during Stanisław August's reign and in its aftermath.

References to Poland, especially in the context of its partitions, can be found in a number of Minerva fictions, even those that are not strictly speaking concerned with the country. Such mentions play the role of temporal contextualisations, and the choice of Poland indicates that the political turmoil there was registered by the Minerva machinery. Poland is also invoked by way of geographical mapping: some Minerva characters go to or return from Poland, others might have relatives or estates there. In Catherine Selden's *Serena* (1800), Poland's having been 'so cruelly dismembered' becomes a topic of conversation.[32] In Mary Charlton's *Phedora; or, the Forest of Minski* (1798), which is set in Livonia, a region that was historically part of the Polish-Lithuanian Commonwealth, one character has been 'driven from Poland by the distractions of that unhappy country'.[33] J. M. H. Hales's *De Willenberg*, an 1821 historical fiction that refers back to the Saxon rule in Poland, defines its timeframe by referring to a time 'when Poland bravely strove to maintain its liberty and independence against the numerous hostilities that environed that unfortunate country'.[34]

As a fully fledged Minerva fiction set in Poland, *De Willenberg* had precedents. *Radzivil, a Romance* (1790) is pitched as 'Translated from the Russ of the Celebrated M. Wocklow', but there is no evidence that the 'celebrated' translator ever existed.[35] The novel tended to be attributed to Mary Ann Radcliffe, sometimes confused with Ann Radcliffe, but this attribution has recently been

---

[32] Catherine Selden, *Serena: A Novel*, 3 vols (London: Minerva, 1800), vol. 2, p. 158.
[33] Charlton, *Phedora*, vol. 1, p. 101.
[34] J. M. H. Hales, *De Willenberg; or, The Talisman. A Tale of Mystery*, 4 vols (London: A. K. Newman, 1821), vol. 1, p. 5.
[35] [Mary Anne Radcliffe?], *Radzivil: A Romance*, 3 vols (London: W. Lane, 1790).

questioned.[36] JoEllen DeLucia prefers to consider it as one of the many publications linked with 'Radcliffe Incorporated', that is, a novel in one way or another linked with the name 'Radcliffe' and thus creating a specific set of associations and expectations.[37] The title of Ann Howell's 1796 *Anzoletta Zadoski* points to one specificity of Minerva Poland – its Italianate character.[38] Thomas Pike Lathy's *The Invisible Enemy; Or, The Mines of Wieliṭska* (1806) continues in this vein and is the most extensive and – arguably – ambitious narrative in this corpus.[39] *De Willenberg* was followed by Francis Lathom's *The Polish Bandit; Or, Who is My Bride?, and Other Tales* (1824), with both publications bearing the imprint of A. K. Newman, in the twilight of the Minerva Press.[40]

The timeframe that these narratives construct – moving from 1790, when the press's specialism was still sentimental fiction, to 1824, when Minerva's gothics had already been written in response to the dominant fashion for the historical romance and manifested a pronounced degree of ironic distance – allows us to see how Poland was utilised by Minerva at varying moments in the life of this publishing house. Reading each of the Poland-centred narratives mentioned, from *Radzivil* to *The Polish Bandit*, this section will underline the salient techniques in the 'gothicisation' of Poland, as well as showing how the country's geographies, both imaginative and factual, contributed to the spatial expansion of Minerva fiction. Proceeding chronologically will help to place these narratives in dialogue with one another and to contextualise them in relation to specific political realities and literary-historical changes, moving from the efflorescence of the gothic, to comic and metafictional tendencies in the first decade of the nineteenth century, and finally to the historical turn in the second.

Radzivil does not offer an elaborate representation of Poland as a setting. Most of the action takes place outside the country, as the exiled and dispossessed

---

[36] Mary Ann Radcliffe features as the author in Montague Summers, *A Gothic Bibliography* (London: The Fortune Press, 1940), p. 136, and Peter Garside, James Raven, and Rainer Schöwerling, *The English Novel 1770–1829: A Bibliographical Survey of Prose Fiction Published in the British Isles. Volume I, 1770–1799* (Oxford: Oxford University Press, 2000), p. 515. In the 2023 update of the latter, Peter Garside, with Jacqueline Belanger, Anthony Mandal, and Sharon Ragaz, problematise this attribution and even suggest that *Radzivil* 'has several marks of being a fairly routine translation possibly from the French', though these 'marks' are not fleshed out. Peter Garside, et al., 'The English Novel, 1800–1829 & 1830–1836. Update 8 (April 2000–June 2023)', *Romantic Textualities: Literature and Print Culture, 1780–1840* 24 (2023): pp. 197–305 (p. 300).

[37] JoEllen DeLucia, 'Radcliffe Incorporated: Ann Radcliffe, Mary Ann Radcliffe and the Minerva Author', *Romantic Textualities: Literature and Print Culture, 1780–1840* 23 (2020): 94–108.

[38] Ann Howell, *Anzoletta Zadoski: A Novel*, 2 vols (London: Minerva, 1796).

[39] Thomas Pike Lathy, *The Invisible Enemy; or, The Mines of Wieliṭska. A Polish Legendary Romance*, 4 vols (London: Minerva, 1806).

[40] Francis Lathom, *The Polish Bandit; Or, Who is My Bride?, and Other Tales* (London: A. K. Newman, 1824).

Radzivil family are making themselves at home near Lausanne to live their pastoral utopia. The motifs of exile and dispossession, as well as the use of the famous family name of Radzivil, suggest an allegorical take on the partitions, which may well be the case, though the eponymous Count Radzivil in this novel is punished for anti-royal sympathies. A probable model for this character would have been Karol Stanisław Radziwiłł (1734–1790), sometimes called the most famous Polish magnate, who was a member of the Bar Confederation, and whose enormous possessions were at one point confiscated following his disobedience towards King Stanisław. Radzivil's role in establishing anti-royal confederations is explained in Coxe's *Travels*, where this 'marshal to all the ... confederacies, united in one formidable association under the appellation of malecontents' is 'arrested in the night by a corps of Russian troops, and sent, without further trial, to Russia [for] a rigorous imprisonment'.[41] The 1790 narrative, as one might expect, does not offer any sustained historical discussion of these contexts – and the exile and dispossession are not eventually followed by a royal pardon, as was the case for the real Radziwiłł – but concludes with sentimental scenes of blissful life in the country, away from the political turmoil. Nor is Count Radzivil the actual protagonist, the novel instead centring on the fortunes and misfortunes of his daughters Julia and Augusta, saved and married by their respective gallants, Henry and Leopold.

In the broader context of the press's take on Gothic Poland, *Radzivil* underlines Minerva's tentative geographical placing of the country in terms of the north-south and east-west axes. In *Inventing Eastern Europe*, Larry Wolff explains how Enlightenment thinkers 'constructed' Eastern Europe and redefined the traditional north-south divide.[42] Wolff quotes a number of eighteenth-century politicians, philosophes, and travel writers, and makes a persuasive point about this major shift in geopolitical identity discourse. Minerva gothics, however, were not uniform in locating Poland in the newly conceived East. Despite the political realities, to which Minerva was responsive, the press cultivated its own conventions and traditions, in a manner reminiscent of how fictional universes are formed and how they evolve. In other words, the pronounced role of southern Europe as the locus for gothic fiction is never completely abandoned in the gothicisation of Poland, which results in a blend of southern and eastern imageries and a convoluted use of vertical and horizontal geographical axes. This quality of Gothic Poland will be most fully explored in Lathy's *The Invisible Enemy*, but *Radzivil* makes for a good starting point to this discussion.

---

[41] William Coxe, *Travels into Poland*, vol. 1, pp. 30–1.
[42] Larry Wolff, *Inventing Eastern Europe: The Map of Civilization on the Mind of the Enlightenment* (Stanford: Stanford University Press, 1994).

The narrative opens with a rather straightforward geographical gesture, situating Poland at the frontier separating the West and the East:

> It was in the concluding year of our late war with the Turks, that a small, but well inhabited town, on the eastern frontiers of Poland, found itself vigorously attacked, by a numerous body of those savage partisans, who hover perpetually round the wings of the Turkish squadrons, and mark the fatal line of their march with a more expanded desolation.[43]

It is unclear which Russo-Turkish war is referred to here, but it is likely to be the 1787–92 struggle, when the Ottoman Empire attempted to reclaim the lands lost to Catherine II in previous decades. Making use of the appeal of contemporaneity, *Radzivil* thus places Poland in the midst of these affairs, at the same time exploring the conventional link between Poland and wars with the Turks that had lingered in the European imagination since Jan III Sobieski's victory over the Ottomans at the battle of Vienna in 1688. Frontier Poland, tormented by 'Tartarian banditti', is not, however, consistently imagined as a gateway to the East.[44] The original Radziwiłł family is here called 'Radzivil Coloni'; the blend uses two ancient family lines, the Radziwiłł and the Colonna, thus indicating Italianate associations with the family's exile and new life in *Pays the Vaud*. As for Poland itself, *Radzivil* does not elaborate on its frontier character beyond the scattered remarks about the Turkish threat and the unsuccessful siege of the Radzivil seat. Poland remains in the sphere of the preconceived imagery of the East, but at the same time becomes absorbed into the cosmopolitan spatial network of the wider south, including Vienna and Lausanne, where most of the action takes place, and imagined Italy, by way of the reader's expectations and implications produced by the Coloni surname.

The Italianate conventions, including naming and setting, are also explored in Howell's *Anzoletta Zadoski*, which is signalled by the title that blends an Italian name with a Polish-sounding surname. Set mostly in England, where mysterious Anzoletta, a Polish exile, finds shelter (through the doings of 'Signior Polletti') and becomes involved in a romantic triangle, the narrative uses Poland as a setting in the interpolated tale of Anzoletta's biological father, Mr Beauchamp, as he recounts his illicit love affair with the daughter of Count Zadoski. The Count's wrath and promise of revenge do not so much affect Beauchamp himself as the fruit of his extramarital affair, who is moved from one place of confinement to another, in various countries, only to be finally saved by her young lover Paget and reunited with her father in England.

---

[43] [Mary Anne Radcliffe?], *Radzivil*, vol. 1, p. 13.
[44] [Mary Anne Radcliffe?], *Radzivil*, vol. 1, p. 14.

The narrative refers to the actual political context, mentioning 'dismembered' and 'enslaved' Poland as a victim to both external influences and internal political instability.[45] The actual representation of the Polish setting – Castle Zadoski on the banks of the Vistula – is cosmopolitan in as much as it is deprived of country-specific features and constructed out of the expected 'gothic' elements:

> This gloomy and desolated fabric was indeed but too characteristic of its superb and haughty master: in many places the fortifications were fallen to decay, and while with Gothic splendor a centinel was posted on the little tower that overlooked the huge portcullis, an enemy might have entered with facility through the breaches which time had made in the walls themselves ... The greater part indeed of this venerable edifice was dismantled of its furniture, and the few habitable apartments presented a memento of the instability of all human grandeur.[46]

Castle Zadoski could be any gothic castle, with the stock imagery of lost splendour, decay, and ruin as exemplified by the passage quoted. That said, the emphasis on 'dismantled furniture' and 'breaches' through which enemies might enter suggests the setting has an allegorical function that can be read as a figure of Poland at the eve of the partitions. Its vulnerability to hostile penetration is also allegorised within the framework of the female gothic: Beauchamp's affair with Zadoski's daughter, also named Anzoletta, his failure to fulfil the promises of marriage, and her pregnancy and fatal lot establish a metaphorical link between the ruined body politic and the abused female body – a trope that would later be explored by Jane Porter in *Thaddeus of Warsaw*, as we shall see.

We learn later on that Count Zadoski conspired against the king and was dispossessed and banished. The motifs of treason and dispossession, familiar from *Radzivil*, are adopted here in a comparable manner. There was clearly a wider tradition of gothic narratives of wrongfully handled property in the period – indeed, questions of inheritance and ownership were central to the gothic from the very beginning[47] – but Minerva's blend of treason and dispossession in the Polish context, as stated before, becomes a geographically specific element grounded in the actual political realities of late eighteenth-century Poland. Fictionalising conspiracies, anti-royal sentiments, and legal and military action against the nobility would have resonated with particular strength in

---

[45] Howell, *Anzoletta Zadoski*, vol. 1, p. 52. [46] Howell, *Anzoletta Zadoski*, vol. 2, pp. 11–12.
[47] See Wolfram Schmidgen, *Eighteenth-Century Fiction and the Law of Property* (Cambridge: Cambridge University Press, 2002), pp. 150–85; Sue Chaplin, *The Gothic and the Rule of Law, 1764–1820* (Basingstoke: Palgrave Macmillan, 2007); Ruth Bienstock Anolik, *Property and Power in English Gothic Literature* (Jefferson: McFarland, 2016).

the 1790s, and the use of Poland, 'a country in the moon', was a safe way to circumvent the troubling context of the French Revolution and its possible impact on British affairs. This politics and poetics of displacement, whereby Poland became a convenient locus for staging wider-ranging concerns in Britain, connects these narratives with the gothic tradition more broadly. David Punter writes about 'a very intense, if displaced, engagement with political and social problems' in the gothic fiction of the 1790s, while Maggie Kilgour points out how these anxieties were moved to 'places geographically and temporally remote', without losing their homely resonance.[48]

The use of conceptual displacement in Poland-set fictions, however, is unstable, as the Poland imagined is not geographically and temporally accurate. While anachronisms are also typical of fictions set elsewhere – Patrick O'Malley has convincingly argued, reading Radcliffe's *Mysteries of Udolpho*, that memory and history are 'shaped by the interests of the present'[49] – temporal obfuscation is accompanied in *Anzoletta Zadoski* by geographical obscurity and misplacement, a strategy that will also be used in later Poland-oriented Minerva gothics. That banished Zadoski finds an asylum in Venice, taking a major leap across unacknowledged Bohemia and Hungary, suggests a false proximity between Poland and Italy, reasserting the novel's familiar, Italianate aspects. This dialectic of factual political and geographical content, on the one hand, and the expected Mediterranean, especially Italian elements, on the other, is explored most fully in Lathy's *The Invisible Enemy; or, The Mines of Wielitska* – the most complex Minerva fiction set in Poland.

Lathy's narrative came out shortly after what Neiman labels the 'zenith' of the Minerva Press (1795–1802), when Lane's imprint was still a major presence in the literary marketplace.[50] It is a lengthy, convoluted narrative, underpinned by the misfortunes of good-natured Leopold and Rhodiska Rosomaski of Castle Vistulof, who are persistently tormented by an invisible enemy – revealed in the final volume as the false pretender to their estate Lanfranco, whom Leopold Rosomaski believes he has killed in self-defence. After a long series of acts of revenge, affecting the Rosomaskis as well as their parents and their children,

---

[48] David Punter, *The Literature of Terror: A History of Gothic Fictions from 1765 to the Present Day*, 2 vols (Harlow: Longman, 1996), p. 54; Maggie Kilgour, *The Rise of the Gothic Novel* (London: Routledge, 1995), p. 23. For a study of the impact of the French Revolution on the British gothic imagination, see Wright, *Britain, France and the Gothic*. For a reading of the early British gothic, especially Clara Reeve and the writers in her wake, in the context of the American Revolution, see James Watt, 'Early British Gothic and the American Revolution', in Angela Wright and Dale Townshend (eds), *The Cambridge History of the Gothic. Volume I: Gothic in the Long Eighteenth Century* (Cambridge: Cambridge University Press, 2020), pp. 243–61.
[49] Patrick R. O'Malley, '"It may be remembered": Spatialized Memory and Gothic History in *The Mysteries of Udolpho*', *The Eighteenth Century* 59:4 (2018): 493–512 (p. 493).
[50] Neiman, *Minerva's Gothics*, pp. 1–46.

Lanfranco reappears as a Miltonic Satan, 'king' of the underground world of the Wielitska (pol. *Wieliczka*) mines, where the revenge scheme comes to its climax, only to be followed by a happy resolution orchestrated by the Rosomaskis' faithful friends shortly afterwards.

The book was duly criticised by the press, as befits this type of publication.[51] Montague Summers, one of the few critics ever to have turned attention to Lathy, quotes two such reviews: the *Critical Review* for November 1806 was 'sorry to find the Mines so unproductive', while the *Monthly Mirror* for January 1807 'dug and dug with that exemplary patience, which by exercise Mr. Lane has so much improved in us, but found no vein of precious ore'.[52] The reviewers' witticisms, creatively playing on the theme of the eponymous mines, are not only critical metaphors; at the same time, they underline what would have been the main subject of interest in Lathy's book. Minerva readers could avail themselves of a number of stories of persecuted innocence, sublime mountains, and ruinous castles, and they might find little that was new in *The Invisible Enemy*. However, the titular Mines of Wielitska, a natural curiosity popularised by Coxe's *Travels into Poland*, would have been the main reason for reading Lathy's narrative, which follows Coxe's closely. Coxe's description embraces a poetics of wonder familiar from more conventional representations of gothic space:

> Many of the excavations or chambers, from whence the salt has been dug, are of an immense size; some are supported with timber, others by vast pillars of salt, which are left standing for that purpose: several of vast dimensions are without any support in the middle. I remarked one of this latter sort in particular, which was certainly 80 feet in height, and so extremely long and broad, as almost to appear amid the subterraneous gloom without limits. The roofs of these vaults are not arched, but flat. The immense size of these chambers, with the spacious passages or galleries, together with the chapels above mentioned, and a few sheds built for the horses which are foddered below, probably gave rise to the exaggerated accounts of some travellers, that these mines contain several villages inhabited by colonies of miners, who never see the light.[53]

Coxe's mentions of 'vast dimensions', 'subterraneous gloom without limits', and 'spacious passages' are taken up and elaborated upon in Lathy's narrative,

---

[51] For a survey of critical responses to Minerva publications, see Megan Peiser, 'William Lane and the Minerva Press in the Review Periodical, 1790–1820', *Romantic Textualities: Literature and Print Culture, 1780–1840* 23 (2020): 124–48.

[52] Quoted after Montague Summers, *The Gothic Quest: A History of the Gothic Novel* (London: The Fortune Press, 1968), pp. 90–1.

[53] Coxe, *Travels into Poland*, vol. 1, p. 198–9.

Figure 4 Johann Esaias Nilson, Wieliczka – Salisfodinae Cracovienses, 1760, The National Museum in Kraków

which also creatively transforms the dismissed suggestion that the mines might be populated into Lanfranco's underground realm. The vastness of the mines, but also their labyrinthine nature, reminiscent of Piranesi's *Carceri*, is also captured in Johann Esaias Nilson's 1760 engraving, which was originally included in a collection of maps of the mines, thus suggesting their complexity and impenetrability (Figure 4).

In a typical Minerva-like manner, with the press promoting its publications across various titles,[54] Lathy's representation of the Polish mines is alluded to in Emma DeLisle's *A Soldier's Offspring* (1810), which includes an interpolated poem, 'Enigma', about the mysteries of nature:

> In Poland some mines I possess,
> From whence no one can ever depart,
> But admiring, they frankly confess,
> I'm a mixture of Nature and Art.[55]

In S. Sykes's *Sir William Dorien* (1811) one character enters Poland and has the dubious pleasure of investigating some mines (though not salt mines this time):

---

[54] For self-promotion techniques, see Neiman, *Minerva's Gothics*, pp. 17–18; Hudson, *Romantic Fiction and Literary Excess in the Minerva Press Era*, pp. 105–6.

[55] Emma DeLisle, *A Soldier's Offspring; or, The Sisters. A Tale*, 2 vols (London: Minerva, 1810), vol. 2, p. 66.

> my miserable destination ... was an iron mine ... At the entrance of this frightful place, my comrades bade me farewell, after delivering me into the hands of the overseer of the miners ... God only knows the sinking of my heart ... when I was let down into the wretched abode of misery and darkness, and fancied that my residence there was doomed to be for life.[56]

The mines are here imagined as a new and alluring variant of the gothic prison, perhaps more effective than familiar edifices in thwarting any hopes of escape. The criticisms quoted by Summers are thus correct in locating the novel's primary appeal, but they miss the metafictional distance that Lathy persistently adopts in his novel, including in his use of the mines.

Summers, disagreeing with the harsh treatment Lathy was receiving, points to his craftsmanship: he 'handles' the typical tropes 'with lavish profusion' and offers a 'first-rate' Lewisite piece of fiction.[57] Lathy is indeed a skilful handler of gothic patterns. He blends the Radcliffean vein with the deadly and hellish gore reminiscent of *The Monk*, as well as playing with peasant-to-nobleman providential discourse and different variants of the gothic plot. In a sense, the first half of the first volume is a coherent and self-contained gothic narrative that sees the rightful owner of the Castle of Vistulof reinstated and married; another fully fledged gothic story is the interpolated tale of one Theresia, imprisoned in a convent upon rejecting a contracted marriage and thus driven to a suicidal act. At one point, Lathy self-reflexively quotes a passage from *King John* about 'wasteful and ridiculous excess', and while the original context is the character sketch of Rhodiska, it is possible to read the quotation as an ironic commentary on excessive fiction-writing such as *The Invisible Enemy* exemplifies. There is a humorously metafictional element to it, too. The novel opens with a Radcliffean 'master-shot':

> Not far from the Carpathian, or, as they are now termed, the Krapac Mountains, which separate Poland from Transylvania, and at the distance of eight leagues from the city of Cracow, there formerly existed an ancient building, called the Castle of Vistulof.[58]

This is followed by what seems to be a self-reflexive exercise in the gothic style: a description of the castle and the surrounding landscape that takes no fewer than eleven pages. This introduction becomes a metafictional nod towards the well-informed reader, and similarly playful uses of conventions abound in the actual narrative, ranging from epic similes and mock-heroic battles in Henry Fielding's vein, to multi-layered stories-within-stories-within-stories, and finally to the preposterous life narratives of villains, bringing to mind the

---

[56] S. Sykes, *Sir William Dorien: A Domestic Story*, 3 vols (London: Minerva, 1812), vol. 3, p. 217.
[57] Summers, *The Gothic Quest*, p. 91.   [58] Lathy, *The Invisible Enemy*, vol. 1, p. i.

dynamic cosmopolitanism of picaresque fiction and the absurdities of *Baron Munschausen*. For example, when the villainous Gramani sojourned in Holland, 'he became Lutheran, Arminian, Calvinist, Arian, Quaker, Jew, Deist, and Atheist, as best served his purpose'.[59] Lathy would have been aware that the original thrill of the early gothic was lost in the first decade of the nineteenth century and that a more playful treatment of the conventions was expected. Summers is right that *The Invisible Enemy* is 'full of first-class thrills',[60] but these are packaged into a narrative whose moods oscillate between terror and horror, on the one hand, and humour, irony, and playfulness, on the other, corroborating Yael Shapira's observation that Minerva gothics are 'deeply heterogeneous' and 'even more frustrating than canonical gothics' in their hybridity.[61]

Given the authorial presence that is strongly felt as one reads through the four volumes of *The Invisible Enemy*, the occasional factual, historical, and geographical tentativeness that characterises this novel, just as it characterised the earlier fictions, should be approached in terms of the writer's strategy. In other words, the seeming discrepancy between temporal and geographical vagueness and Italianate conventions, on the one hand, and the factual content, including proper names and specific loci, on the other, should be reconciled and read as premeditated. *The Invisible Enemy* sustains the allure of Minerva's southern European universe, but enriches it with country-specific elements in a manner that exceeds the use of the actual Polish content in *Radzivil* and *Anzoletta Zadoski*. In Lathy's narrative Poland is still 'filtered' through the typical imagery based on the work of Radcliffe and Salvator Rosa, but the conventional necessities of spatial representation are complemented not only with correctly located towns and cities, some of which are obscure – such as Jarosław or Żabno – but also, as we have seen, with a skilful foregrounding of the Mines of Wielitska.

The mines are absorbed into the spatial universe through literary means: the labyrinthine underground spaces are familiar from representations of gothic edifices, such as castles, abbeys, and the prisons of the Inquisition (a hall 'hung all over with black'), while also bringing to mind Miltonic hell. Lanfranco, the villain, is endowed with Satanic qualities, and combines aspects of Milton's antihero and Lewis's Ambrosio. At one point we read about how 'Lanfranco rolled his inflamed eyes; his countenance exhibited fury and phrenzy; the veins of his forehead and temples were swollen; his cheeks were on fire; his parched lips frothed; he was horrible to the aspect'.[62] This excess of horror in character

---

[59] Lathy, *The Invisible Enemy*, vol. 3, p. 264. [60] Summers, *The Gothic Quest*, p. 91.
[61] Yael Shapira, 'Isabella Kelly and the Minerva Gothic Challenge', *Romantic Textualities: Literature and Print Culture, 1780–1840* 23 (2020): 168–84 (p. 169).
[62] Lathy, *The Invisible Enemy*, vol. 4, p. 127.

representation is reminiscent of Lewis's focus on facial expression and Milton's parallels between hellish spaces and 'inflamed' thoughts.[63]

At the same time, however, the mines are presented in an informative manner, with the narrative voice recounting their history and way of functioning, mainly through references to Coxe's *Travels into Poland*, both implicit and explicit. The manner in which the mines are introduced, in fact, reconciles the cognitive appeal of travel writing with the thrill of gothic romance: 'Of this grand phenomenon of natural history, it will be also proper to give the following short sketch, to enable those who may be unacquainted with it, to penetrate into the dark scenes which the unfortunate Rosomaskis were yet doomed to go through.'[64] This mode is also adopted shortly afterwards, as the gothic qualities of the mines are connected with specific political circumstances:

> If left to himself, he [i.e. a visitor] would be in danger of losing himself in the multitude of subterraneous roads, galleries, or streets, which intersect each other, and form a sort of very intricate labyrinth.— This precaution is now the more necessary, because, since the House of Austria has been in possession of this treasure, the officers of the mines have been strictly ordered not to communicate in future any plan of the mines.[65]

The mines thus differ from the seat of Radzivil or Castle Zadoski in as much as they are not gothic by virtue of conceptual representation – as a frontier or a space vulnerable to hostile penetration; they are essentially gothic, with Poland now absorbed into the Minerva universe not just nominally, by way of the press's self-reproduction, spatial expansion, and cosmopolitan character, but substantially, as its 'wonder of nature' enriches the gothic universe just as Alpine caverns and chasms did before. Lathy's representation of the mines thus adds to the discourse of the gothic sublime: 'these [subterranean abysses] contained a vast mine of salt, which the bowels of the Carpathian mountains concealed, and which appear to have been deposited there from time immemorial by the residence of the sea'.[66] Sublimity is here hinted at through what we would now call a deep time perspective, while the metaphor of 'the bowels' of the mountains suggests a hellish function that these spaces will perform, opening up the Miltonic imagery that is otherwise implemented in this context.

---

[63] Compare with Satan's arrival in hell, 'with thoughts inflamed of highest design', John Milton, *Paradise Lost*, intr. Philip Pullman (Oxford: Oxford University Press, 2005), pp. 62–3; and the following encounter between Ambrosio and Antonia: 'His eyes rolled fearfully: Antonia trembled, whenever She met their gaze. He seemed to meditate on something horrible . . . .' Matthew Gregory Lewis, *The Monk*, intr. Stephen King (Oxford: Oxford University Press, 2002), p. 386.
[64] Lathy, *The Invisible Enemy*, vol. 4, pp. 86–7.   [65] Lathy, *The Invisible Enemy*, vol. 4, p. 91.
[66] Lathy, *The Invisible Enemy*, vol. 4, p. 86.

The mines in *The Invisible Enemy* also perform a crucial metafictional function, metonymically capturing Lathy's playful use of the false proximity between Italy and Poland on which his novel depends, as did the previous examples discussed. Lathy sustains the Italianate character of Poland through the typical use of Italianised Polish names (such as Lanfranco, Lodowico) and through setting a substantial part of the narrative in Genoa, as the Rosomaskis are forced by their invisible enemy to leave Poland. While a reader seasoned in gothic descriptions of the Alpine passage would clearly expect more, the journey merits only a brief acknowledgement:

> In this state of horrible anxiety, the Rosomaskis were hurried along for seven days, and an equal number of nights, successively. At last the carriage stopped, and they were ordered to alight. One of the banditti then addressed them in these words—
> '... The road before you leads to Genoa, from which city you are not far distant. That is the place which he who is the arbiter of your fate, has fixed upon for your exile, which is to continue for life. If you ever should seek to quit it, tremble for your lives.'[67]

Covering the distance of around 1300 kilometres in 7 days indeed qualifies for the exiles to be considered to be 'hurried along', but more importantly, it is also the reader that is hurried along, deprived of the typical narrative of the passage, especially as Lathy does not otherwise avoid landscape descriptions, as we have seen. The page-turning quality is one thing; the suspension of the actual distance between the two countries is another.

This suspension comes to the fore later on, as Lanfranco is eventually provoked to resume his villainy when the Rosomaskis are too close to establishing a comfortable living for themselves in exile. The parties involved cover the distance with a similar narrative ease, but as the climax that is meant to take place in the mines of Wielitska approaches, Lathy's villain uses a method of deception that gains in metafictional significance in the wider context of Minerva's Italy-like Poland: the imprisoned Rosomaskis are fooled into believing that they are confined in Lanfranco's castle by Lake Garda, with the link between the mines and the imagery of the gothic castle thus reasserted. When the villain decides to send Rhodiska back to Cracow, he adopts a stratagem that is meant to sustain the deception by maintaining a false geographical distance: 'We will send her to Cracow, with such precautions as will not let her entertain a doubt that she has performed the length of way requisite to bring her thither from my fictitious castle on the shores of the lake of Guarda. We shall thus escape suspicion ... '.[68] The stratagem is then duly accounted for:

---

[67] Lathy, *The Invisible Enemy*, vol. 2, pp. 144–5.   [68] Lathy, *The Invisible Enemy*, vol. 4, p. 164.

> The coachman, who had received his instructions, instead of taking the road to Cracow, conducted the berlin into one of those immense forests, which then bristled the greatest part of Poland: that to which he drove the berlin, was about ten leagues in length, and extended from the Carpathian mountains to the town of Byecz. As soon as the coachman arrived at the other extremity of the forest, he turned about and drove back again; he stopped only such time as was strictly necessary to refresh the horses, or to get fresh ones, which were continually brought to him at a particular spot, which had been fixed upon for that purpose ... After having traversed the forest six times in different directions, they made the circuit of it, and so continued this tortuous and serpentine march, without having ever left the forest; till having passed five days and nights in the journey, they had taken all the precautions necessary to persuade Rhodiska that she had made a voyage of two hundred leagues, which is nearly the distance from the lake of Guarda to Cracow.[69]

Lanfranco's method has a metafictional significance as the trick against Rhodiska parallels the deceptive machinery of *The Invisible Enemy*, and Minerva in general, as far as spatial representation is concerned. The actual distance between Poland and Italy – geographical, cultural, and political – is compromised, producing an effect of obfuscation that need not be read as an outcome of the authors' limited knowledge about the 'country in the moon'. As we have seen, factual details about Poland are scattered across the Minerva universe, but this content is introduced along with the familiar conventions, thus facilitating readability and strengthening the cross-textual identity of the Minerva productions. Conceived of as such, with the assumption that an impenetrably 'dark' (literally and metaphorically) forest separates Cracow from the Italian Alps, Poland is not only seen as a reference point in the North-South divide but actually placed in the gothic south, with the expansive and unmapped network of underground passages spreading out of the mines and creating the illusion that they might be reaching much further than Cracow and the Carpathian mountains. As Lathy's source text, Coxe's *Travels*, has it:

> the best judges on the spot suppose, with the greatest appearance of probability, this solid body of salt to branch into various directions, the extent of which cannot be known: of that part which has been perforated, the depth is only calculated as far as they have hitherto dug; and who can ascertain how much farther it may descend?[70]

The Invisible Enemy thus offers a meta-commentary on how Gothic Poland became a theme in Minerva gothics. At the same time, in a manner comparable to *Radzivil* and *Anzoletta Zadoski*, it explores the gothic potential of the history

---

[69] Lathy, *The Invisible Enemy*, vol. 4, pp. 169–71.
[70] Coxe, *Travels into Poland*, vol. 1, pp. 197–8.

of partitions through allegorisation. While the other two narratives focused on conspiracies and dispossession, Lathy's lengthy and episodic narrative of Lanfranco tormenting three generations of a Polish family gains in figurative meaning when the villain reaches Italy under the false name of Dolgorucki. Yuri Dolgorukiy (d. 1157), Grand Prince of Kiev, was the legendary founder of Moscow. The Dolgorukis were also an influential family in the eighteenth century, with representatives in the Tsarist military and diplomacy, some of whom were active in Poland during the Russo-Polish wars and in their aftermath. To Lathy, the Dolgoruki name would have offered a generic potential with imperialist undertones, thus suggesting that the stratagems of Lanfranco against a Polish family can be read as a political allegory about tormented Poland.

Given the metafictive inventiveness of Lathy's book, the later Minerva fictions set in Poland – *De Willenberg* and *The Polish Bandit* – may disappoint in as much as they contribute very little beyond the already established imagery. *De Willenberg* is the familiar story of a love quadruple, featuring characters (with German-sounding names) who move between courts, convents, and castles in central Poland. One of them is King Augustus, and while the German context might suggest that the timeframe of the events covers the reign of the Saxon dynasty in Poland – Augustus II and Augustus III – the idealised sovereign in *De Willenberg* would probably have made readers think of Stanisław August. The temporal hint at the beginning of the novel is deliberately vague:

> In one of those memorable battles when Poland bravely strove to maintain its liberties and independence against the numerous hostilities that environed that unfortunate country, the javelin of a Cossack was furiously aimed at the bosom of the royal Augustus, then sovereign and leader of the Polish armies.[71]

Augustus is saved and returns triumphantly to Warsaw to celebrate Poland's victory; the details regarding the military conflict are shrouded in obscurity, so that the implied setting in the distant past could correspond to or bring to mind the more immediate struggles of the 1790s. This possibility is reinforced when shortly afterwards we read about 'the Russian invaders and their allies', while king Augustus is idealised as the monarch whose only ambition was to save 'a suffering and persecuted nation, and uphold his tottering country'.[72]

In Lathom's 'The Polish Bandit', which is the first tale in his collection, and the only one set in Poland, the fictional timeframe has a similar function:

> The period at which our tale opens, is towards the close of the sixteenth century, when Stanislaus, king of Poland, having long waged a tedious and

---

[71] Hales, *De Willenberg*, vol. 1, p. 5.   [72] Hales, *De Willenberg*, vol. 1, p. 15; 25.

unsuccessful war against the emperor of Russia, had resolved to head his troops in person, and make a desperate effort to penetrate into the dominions of his enemy.[73]

The Polish-Lithuanian Commonwealth at that time was one of the most powerful states in Europe, but it was not engaged in an 'unsuccessful' war against Russia, and it was not ruled by a king named Stanislaus. A seasoned writer in the Radcliffean vein, Lathom does exactly what Radcliffe had done with respect to sixteenth-century France and Italy in *The Mysteries of Udolpho*: the historical reference serves a conventional function of imagining the obscure 'gothic' past, while the actual temporal context is the present.

'The Polish Bandit' features the good-natured Stanislaus as a *deus ex machina*-like character who facilitates a happy resolution by pardoning the protagonists' misdemeanours. In *De Willenberg*, Augustus does the same, but first has a bigger role to play: he is involved in a romantic quadruple, as his decision to take Victoria as his queen is compromised by his rivals: his scheming brother Leopold and the knightly De Willenberg – the protagonist of the novel. De Willenberg and Victoria's unfulfilled love takes them through the convent, a banditti castle, and the Consistory prison and culminates on the scaffold, where they are saved by a royal pardon and finally united. The king's unsuccessful attempt at taking 'Victoria' for his wife, as well as Leopold's anti-royal conspiracy, invites allegorical readings, though *De Willenberg* for the most part remains a popular and immersive blend of Scottian and Radcliffean aesthetics that recycles familiar tropes. Lathom was probably responding to *De Willenberg* in his tale, adopting similar motifs and plot structures: the quadruple, anti-royal conspiracies, confused identities, dispossession, and the German-sounding name of the knightly protagonist, Hermandorff, which recalls Victoria's family name, Herman. Both narratives, and especially *De Willenberg*, are testimonies to the 'historical' turn in gothic writing after the success of *Waverley* in 1814, and document the impact of this type of fiction on gothic writing in the 1820s.[74]

The crafty though repetitive writing of these fictions translates into the construction of Gothic Poland. In *De Willenberg*, the architectural settings do not go beyond the established conventions: they are skilfully described, with a tinge of poetic spirit, but deprived of Lathy's meta-discourse that would encourage the reader to search for meanings beneath the pleasing surface. Victoria's home – Castle Herman – recycles magnificence, lost splendour, ivy decorations, and Radcliffean views from the window; the banditti castle is larger than life in its gothic qualities; while the convent and the Consistory prison are more 'Lewisite' than their likely models in *The Monk*. The condensed

---

[73] Lathom, *The Polish Bandit*, p. 12. [74] Potter, *The History of Gothic Publishing*, pp. 6–7.

narrative of 'The Polish Bandit', in turn, does not allow for excessive descriptions, but the hints that we are given about the convent of the Blessed Cross, where most of the action takes place, and the aristocratic estates mentioned by way of accounting for the family backgrounds of the characters involved, do not go beyond the familiar and the expected.

The addition to this self-reproductive spatial imagery in both fictions is the forest surrounding the architectural establishments, or indeed 'almost envelop[ing]' them, as we read in *De Willenberg*.[75] As we shall see, the Polish forest was creatively elaborated upon in later fiction, including by Catherine Gore, and was also adopted in related Minerva gothics, such as the already mentioned *Phedora; or, the Forest of Minski*. In *De Willenberg* the forest is the dark in-between zone that separates the mapped spaces:

> an ancient and extensive forest, ... it was universally known to be dangerous to every traveller that ventured into its frightful and intricate labyrinths, many parts of it preserving the darkness of midnight, and especially from the formidable bands of marauders that infested its secret caverns and recesses. So general were the prejudice and terror existing against it, that it had long received the signal appellation of the Forest of Death. None dared reside in its vicinity, and all those who did live nearest, scrupulously avoided advancing a step further towards it, always taking a circuitous road, whenever they had occasion to go to their town.[76]

The Forest of Death, however, is reduced to a gothic simulacrum, losing its connection with any purported subject of representation; as Jerrold Hogle argues within the framework of his 'counterfeit' theory, 'Gothic figures ... are always signs of other signs'.[77] While Lathy's mines were particularised, the forest in *De Willenberg* is universalised through Minerva's cosmopolitan conventions: as De Willenberg is searching for shelter during a storm, when the ominous tree branches seem as if on fire when illuminated by violent lightning, he is accosted by banditti who speak Italian to him.[78] The later part of the novel explains how the Tuscan bandits ended up in central Poland, but in this particular forest scene the use of Italian does not raise an eyebrow – as if it were expected that the Masovian forest would be infested by Italian-speaking ruffians led by Ferdinand Velasco and occupying an otherwise unknown castle hidden by the thick foliage. The forest is further aligned with Salvator Rosa-style imagery through rock-and-cliff

---

[75] Hales, *De Willenberg*, vol. 2, p. 25.   [76] Hales, *De Willenberg*, vol. 2, pp. 6–7.
[77] Jerrold E. Hogle, 'Abjection as Gothic and the Gothic as Abjection', in Jerrold E. Hogle and Robert Miles (eds) *The Gothic and Theory: An Edinburgh Companion* (Edinburgh: Edinburgh University Press, 2019), pp. 108–126 (p. 119).
[78] Hales, *De Willenberg*, vol. 2, p. 162; 171.

embellishments that could not be encountered in Masovian plains, which in reality are characterised by flat rural terrain:

> A chain of rocks on either side now bounded the road, forming a long narrow defile, overhung in many places by the projecting cliffs, and in others by the tall firs and pines that grew at their base, so closely intermingled, that even the vivid lightning, which still continued to illuminate the face of the heavens, could not penetrate them.[79]

De Willenberg's forest is abstract and cosmopolitan, constituted by the poetics of repetition, obfuscation, and spatial ambiguity. It is a copy of a copy and does not particularise the setting.

In 'The Polish Bandit', rather than becoming an allegorical simulacrum, the forest is the only geographically specific locale, bringing to mind *The Invisible Enemy*'s use of actual Polish settings – the Wielitska salt mines – for the expansion of gothic spatial imagery. A haunt of banditti, like in *De Willenberg*, the forest here is concretised as 'the forest of Palutski' (rather than being allegorised as 'the Forest of Death'), but why Lathom would choose the region of Pałuki (in Greater Poland) as the setting for his tale remains a mystery. The only other Polish-sounding proper name is that of the archbishop of Wilitski, who absolves the tale's heroine of her premature monastic vows, but that name does not shed any further light on the meanings behind the use of Pałuki, being, most probably, a variant of Wielitska, which would have been familiar to readers thanks to Coxe and Lathy.

The only well-informed and accurate insertion of a Polish proper name in Lathom's tale, the forest of Palutski is endowed with a meta-discursive function, illustrating the actual use of Polish settings in the Minerva universe. Nevertheless, *De Willenberg*'s non-specific 'Forest of Death' performs this function too, exemplifying the broader spatial mechanics at play. The universalised extension of space, connecting and merging Poland and Salvator Rosa-like Italy, depends on conceptual shrinking: when we become acquainted with the background story of the forest banditti, we learn that upon leaving Tuscany they arrived in central Poland in merely three days. If the seven-day passage from Genoa to Cracow meant being 'hurried along' in *The Invisible Enemy*, *De Willenberg* further reduces this distance, and, needless to say – like in *Anzoletta Zadoski* – there is no mention of what the bandits passed through in between their old and new homes. This shrinking also characterises the fragmented idea of Poland as a setting. As we have seen, the Masovian plains are endowed with mountainous elements. At one point, as De Willenberg, like Radcliffe's sensitive heroes, is taking advantage of the vista offered by one of the hills, he enjoys a highly improbable prospect: 'he turned on

---

[79] Hales, *De Willenberg*, vol. 2, pp. 174–5.

a path that wound up the side of an immense chain of towering and gigantic rocks, the highest of which overtopped the tallest trees, and commanded a far-distant view of the Baltic and its magnificent shores'.[80]

Such lapses, however, very much like the historical inaccuracies, should not be read as testimonies to ignorance. It takes but one cursory look at the map of Europe to understand the distance separating the Baltic, the Warsaw area, and the Polish mountains. The fictional blending of these geographical regions, just like the suspension of the distance between Poland and Italy, and indeed, the uncertainty regarding the location of Poland with respect to the north-south and east-west axes, which I have already addressed, are all elements of the broader agenda determining the autonomous, as it were, formation of the Minerva spatial imagery that the different examples discussed here document. What *The Invisible Enemy* does through its spatial trick, which, as we have seen, gains in metafictional significance, *De Willenberg* suggests through a minor detail that captures the spatial poetics at play and can serve as an apt concluding illustration of what Minerva authors made of Poland.

When De Willenberg is marvelling at the beauties of the Polish landscape, the multisensory experience is amplified by what he understands to be 'the glory of the Omnipotent Being' and his 'wonderful works':

> the sky was perfectly serene, and the lower air was filled with the delicious perfume of the most odoriferous plants, which flourished there spontaneously; the sweet-scented clematis, the oleander, and the agnus cactus, in full bearing, threw their fragrance around, and their beautifully-varied colours feasted the eye . . . .[81]

The clematis, the oleander, and the agnus cactus – the three plants 'perfuming' and 'colouring' Gothic Poland in Minerva fiction – become metaphors of the spatial poetics. While some species of the clematis are native to Poland, among other countries, the oleander is typically a Mediterranean plant, and the agnus cactus grows in the Mediterranean and in the Near East. The three flowers could not have been seen enriching the wild Polish scenery, but put together they capture Minerva's blending of the various spatial preconceptions regarding Poland and its potential usefulness for the gothic genre. Minerva fed on the factual content regarding the dismembered country, popularised by Coxe and others, and adjusted it to match the prevalent Italianate imagery, as well as exploring and recycling the attractive conceptualisations of Poland as a frontier country, a gateway to the Near East. The 'historical turn' in the aftermath of Scott's phenomenal success in 1814 did not result in a greater sensitivity to historical detail, nor in accuracy of representation, but would have encouraged Minerva authors to capitalise further

---

[80] Hales, *De Willenberg*, vol. 2, p. 252. [81] Hales, *De Willenberg*, vol. 2, p. 254.

on the recognisability of King Stanisław August as a historical figure. While the representations of Poland in Porter's *Thaddeus of Warsaw* and Gore's *Polish Tales* depart from the Italianate fashion, and are largely independent of Minerva's fixed spatial conventions, they creatively elaborate on the multi-layered construct of Gothic Poland already established.

2 Jane Porter's *Thaddeus of Warsaw* (1803): Poland and the Gothic Underplots

Jane Porter's *Thaddeus of Warsaw* was published by Longman and Rees in 1803. It was not Porter's first publication, but the first with 'Miss Porter' on the title page, which the publisher apparently considered to be a way to boost sales. The novel tells the story of Thaddeus Constantine Sobieski – a Polish nobleman of an (absent) English father, descendent of King Jan III Sobieski by way of his mother Therese Sobieski, a soldier during the Polish-Russian war of 1792 and the Kosciuszko Uprising of 1794, and an exile in London, where he eventually starts a new life and is reunited with his once rakish father. While the name of Thaddeus brings to mind General Tadeusz Kościuszko – and indeed Porter was writing the novel amidst what has been termed 'the Kościuszko craze' in British Romanticism – the hero is in fact a fictional construct, combining the ancient heritage of the Sobieski family with the international fame of Kościuszko at the end of the eighteenth century. Francis Zapatka, writing about how 'this excitement was expressed in verse, prose fiction, and published correspondence and diaries', locates the phenomenon in the period 1794–1826 (as documented by the corpus of his materials).[82] This suggests that the 'gothicisation' of Poland discussed in this Element was a concomitant phenomenon, and that the role of Kościuszko – as a historical figure and as a myth of heroism – in orienting public interest towards the dismembered country must not be underestimated. In this section, I will argue that Porter responded to the fall of Poland by deploying female gothic underplots, which she allegorised to ponder more general matters concerning the interrelatedness of the female body and the body politic. It will also demonstrate how Porter's early experiences as a gothic writer eventually translated into her handling of the Polish question amidst 'the Kościuszko craze', despite the writer's marked departure from gothic fiction.

Porter's interest in the Polish cause – or, more appropriately, the gradual fall of the Polish-Lithuanian Commonwealth in the late eighteenth century – was triggered by several factors. She was involved in the military-artistic projects of her brother Robert, a painter of battle scenes; she would have followed news of the Polish revolution and its aftermath in 1792–5, and the injured Kościuszko's visit to London in 1797. She would have learned about Poland from William

---

[82] Zapatka, 'Kościuszko among the English Romantics', p. 255.

Figure 5 Anthony Cardon, after Richard Cosway, General Thaddeus Kościuszko, 1 January 1798.Courtesy of the John Carter Brown Library at Brown University

Coxe's *Travels* and Stephen Jones's *History*, of which there is textual evidence in the novel, and she would have read some of the Kościuszko- and Poland-related poetry of the time, almost certainly going beyond the verses composed by her sister Anna Maria – 'O! Freedom! Valour! Resignation! Here / Pay to your godlike son the sacred tear . . .' – that were used in an engraved copy of Richard Cosway's famous painting of Kościuszko in London (Figure 5). Porter also had broader interests in heroic figures and persecuted nations, and just as the fame of Kościuszko and the fall of Poland were creatively fictionalised in *Thaddeus of Warsaw*, so Scottish heroes, such as William Wallace, and their lost struggles for independence, provided an incentive for her subsequent work of historical fiction, *The Scottish Chiefs* (1810).[83]

---

[83] Devoney Looser discusses the influence of war hero Sidney Smith on Porter and her historical fiction, showing how the writer constructed a proto 'Great Man' theory, which would later on be systematised by Thomas Carlyle. See Devoney Looser, 'The Great Man and Women's Historical Fiction: Jane Porter and Sir Sidney Smith', *Women's Writing* 19:3 (2012): 293–314.

Enormously successful upon publication,[84] then largely forgotten, and now a subject of renewed critical attention, *Thaddeus of Warsaw* is not typically studied in the context of the gothic tradition, as shall be undertaken in this section. Instead, critics tend to underline this work's role in the shaping of the form of the historical novel, something Jane Porter would have embraced.[85] After the success of Walter Scott's fiction, in the preface to the revised edition of *Thaddeus* (1831) that appeared in the Colburn and Bentley *Standard Novels* series, Porter reminds readers about her own pioneering role in the development of this type of fiction. She explains her method of combining historical characters and events with an element of fiction, and considers her work a 'new species of writing', later imitated:

> [Scott] did me the honour to adopt the style or class of novel of which 'Thaddeus of Warsaw' was the first:— a class which, uniting the personages and facts of real history or biography, with a combining and illustrative machinery of the imagination, formed a new species of writing in that day.[86]

Critics such as Thomas McLean, Fiona Price, and Devoney Looser, among others, have undertaken significant work over the recent two decades to reinstate Porter in the canon of nineteenth-century historical fiction, invariably underlining that her groundbreaking contribution preceded Scott's narratives. At the same time, they have been mindful of the generic complexity of *Thaddeus of Warsaw*, which was also signalled by Porter, who in the preface to the 1803 edition suggested her indebtedness both to the domestic fiction of Richardson and to grand biographical writing, with its allegorical potential.[87] McLean's generic labels range from *Thaddeus* being a compound of 'a continental romance' and 'an English domestic novel' to 'a mix of historical romance, social comedy and critical commentary on Britain's treatment of foreign exiles'.[88] These claims are indeed apt indications of the formal shape of Porter's historical novel.

---

[84] For example, the *Critical Review* points out: 'Miss Porter has availed herself of a very interesting period in history for the foundation of her tale. Often have we felt our heart rent by indignation and pity, at the dismemberment of Poland and the cruel fate of Stanislaus. Truth and fiction are blended with much propriety in these volumes; and we have turned with sincere pleasure to the pages that praise the valour of Kosciuszko; and recount, though but as a novel, the adventures of a Sobieski'. *The Critical Review* 39 (1803): 120. This review was included in several editions of *Thaddeus* and reprinted across contemporary magazines.

[85] Thomas McLean, 'Nobody's Argument: Jane Porter and the Historical Novel', *Journal for Early Modern Cultural Studies* 7:2 (2007): 88–103; McLean, *The Other East*, pp. 66–78; Price, *Reinventing Liberty*, pp. 124–5; 170.

[86] Jane Porter, *Thaddeus of Warsaw*, rev. ed. (London: Henry Colburn and Richard Bentley, 1831), p. vi.

[87] Jane Porter, *Thaddeus of Warsaw* (London: T. N. Longman and O. Rees, 1803), pp. vii–x.

[88] McLean, *The Other East*, pp. 66–87; Thomas McLean, 'Introduction', in Jane Porter, *Thaddeus of Warsaw*, edited by Thomas McLean and Ruth Knezevic (Edinburgh: Edinburgh University Press, 2022), pp. viii–xxiii (p. viii)

When she reasserted her pioneering role in the development of the historical novel in the 1831 preface, Porter thought it fit to distance herself from the gothic tradition, writing that her work was 'different' to 'the wildly interesting romances of Anne [*sic*] Radcliffe, whose magical wonders and mysteries were then the ruling style of the day'.[89] This claim for the purported 'seriousness' of her literary project finds an earlier equivalent in her personal diary, where in an entry for 13–20 January 1801 she recalls the 'torture' of sociable readings of gothic 'trash': 'hour after hour spent in wading through pages of sheeted ghosts, and goblins dire'.[90] When after the publication of her second successful novel, *The Scottish Chiefs*, Porter's celebrity would have encouraged her to curate her public persona as an author with particular care, it was typical of the biographical sketches published in popular magazines, likely with the author's own editorial attention, to consider Thaddeus her 'first' novel and omit her beginnings as a gothic writer.[91] Porter's break with the gothic is also noted by Looser, for whom the *Thaddeus* project was a 'turning point' in the writing career of an author of gothic and oriental fictions, 'demonstrating her changing conception and presentation of herself as an author'.[92] In line with Porter herself, Looser separates the author's groundbreaking achievements from the gothic: *Thaddeus*, given its critical and popular success, is seen as testimony to her transformation as a writer and published author.

The Spirit of the Elbe (1799), the gothic novel mentioned by Looser, was credited with a potential to 'afford entertainment', as the reviewer for the *Critical Review* put it,[93] and was even adapted for the ballet by Charles Dibdin as *Blackenberg; or, Spirit of the Elbe*, the description of which designates the source text as 'a popular novel'.[94] Nevertheless, at the peak of Radcliffean fashions, it did not rank among the most successful gothic romances of the time. Porter's gothic competence, however, proved useful, as I will argue in what follows, when she turned to late eighteenth-century Polish history in the first volume of *Thaddeus of Warsaw*. Her transition from gothic to historical writing was smoother than she would have admitted, and reveals patterns of continuity rather than a radical turn. This, perhaps inadvertently, was suggested

---

[89] Porter, *Thaddeus of Warsaw* (1831), p. xi.
[90] Quoted after Looser, *Sister Novelists: The Trailblazing Porter Sisters, Who Paved the Way for Austen and the Brontës* (London: Bloomsbury, 2022), Epub ebook, ch. 5.
[91] Looser, *Sister Novelists*, ch. 16.
[92] Looser, 'The Great Man and Women's Historical Fiction', p. 293.
[93] *The Critical Review* 26 (1799): 357.
[94] Charles Dibdin, 'Explanatory Sketch of the new Serious Pantomime of Blackenberg; or, The Spirit of the Elbe', in *Songs, &c. in the Burletta of the Bird Catcher: Or, Catch as Catch Can. With a Copious Description of the Story of the New Pantomime of Peter Wilkins: or, Harlequin in the Flying World. And Also of the New Splendid Ballet Spectacle of Blackenberg; or, Spirit of the Elbe. As Performed at Sadler's Wells* (London, 1800), np.

> This day was published,
> In Four Volumes, price 14s. in boards,
> THADDEUS of WARSAW; a NOVEL.
> By Miſs PORTER.
> Printed for T. N. Longman and O. Rees, Paternoſter-row.
> Of whom may be had,
> 1. The SPIRIT of the ELBE; a Romance; in three Volumes. Price 9s. boards.
> 2. OCTAVIA; a Novel; by Anna Maria Porter, in three Vols. Price 10s. 6d. boards.

Figure 6 A clipping from The Star, 4 April 1803, The British Newspaper Archive

by Longman and Rees, who decided to promote the publication of *Thaddeus* by pairing this novel with *The Spirit of the Elbe*, which was also their publication, in an advertisement published in *The Star* newspaper (4 April 1803, Figure 6).

Porter's debut novel, *The Spirit of the Elbe* was for the author a training ground in the possibilities of the female gothic.[95] It is moderately successful, and clearly indebted to Ann Radcliffe, despite the nominal reliance on the German *Schauerroman* (suggested by a German quotation on the title page and the Saxon setting) and the use, albeit restrained, of the unexplained supernatural. The author's first idea for the title was 'Mysteries of the Black Forest', establishing a link with *The Mysteries of Udolpho* and *The Romance of the Forest*, and underlining the geographical inconsistencies of the Radcliffean gothic: the Black Forest is in a completely different part of Germany than Saxony. At the same time, the first and the final ideas for the title equally suggest that while Porter's work was printed by a respectable press, she would have intended her gothic novel to be viewed in the context of popular Minerva publications such as Karl Friedrich Kahlert's *The Necromancer: Or the Tale of the Black Forest* (1794) and *The Orphan of the Rhine* by Eleanor Sleath (1798), both of which were included in Isabella Thorpe's list of 'horrid' novels in *Northanger Abbey*. Work on *The Spirit of the Elbe*, as Looser relates, was preceded by the author's exposure to Mary Wollstonecraft's proto-feminist thought and Porter's editorial work on an unpublished manuscript featuring

---

[95] I am aware of the contentiousness of the term 'female gothic', but I nevertheless deploy the category as an apt methodological tool for uncovering Porter's investment in the gothic in *Thaddeus of Warsaw*. For a synthesis of the debate surrounding the term, as well as its adaptability to new critical contexts, see Angela Wright, *Gothic Fiction: A Reader's Guide to Essential Criticism* (Basingstoke: Palgrave Macmillan, 2007), pp. 125–30, and Diana Wallace and Andrew Smith, 'Introduction: Defining the Female Gothic', in Diana Wallace and Andrew Smith (eds), *The Female Gothic: New Directions* (Basingstoke: Palgrave Macmillan, 2009), pp. 1–12. Diana Wallace's criticism, in particular, has shown how the 'female gothic' as a category of reading can bridge the gap between the gothic and women's historical fiction. See Diana Wallace, *The Woman's Historical Novel British Women Writers, 1900–2000* (Basingstoke: Palgrave Macmillan, 2005), p. 3.

Wollstonecraft's ghost. At the time Porter was also inclined towards writing imitations of Mary Robinson and Hannah More, and the former became a mentor figure to Porter. Her interest in the gothic would have also been related to her gradual recognition of the endangered female body – something she experienced herself when kissed against her will by a military man, an episode she reports with disgust in a letter to her sister Maria.[96]

Rosamund, the heroine of Porter's debut, is a typical damsel in distress, tormented by a wicked aunt and a tyrannical uncle, Count Blackenberg, the unlawful owner of the Castle of Koningstein, where the action takes place. Orphaned and brought up in a convent, she is taken into the castle, where she discovers its dark mysteries and falls victim to mental and physical violence from the villainous uncle. Volume 2 of the novel is a gender reversal narrative, introducing the character of Theodore, another orphan victimised by Blackenberg. He is endowed with stereotypically effeminate features: he is subject to swooning and sobbing, and is labelled 'a little womanish'.[97] Porter doubles her narrative by imperilling Theodore and placing him in the room previously occupied by Rosamund, before disclosing his true identity as Sigismund, the true inheritor of the castle, long considered dead. Volume 3 sees the villain punished and dying, while Sigismund is declared the rightful inheritor of the castle and reunited with his mother (who was also believed to be dead). Rosamund is predictably saved by the newly reinstated hero, and the couple's union concludes the romance.

The Spirit of the Elbe reveals several conceptual, formal, and thematic links with *Thaddeus of Warsaw*. The first is the doubled narrative design, whereby the female gothic narrative featuring Rosamund is followed by the story of Sigismund, another orphan, who reconciles a conventional heroic character with a tinge of femininity. This twofold narrative structure characterises *Thaddeus*, too, where the story of victimised Therese Sobieski is later complemented – indeed, uncannily doubled to some extent – by the account of orphaned Thaddeus's fortunes and misfortunes as an exile in London. Thaddeus, in a similar manner to Sigismund, combines heroism with an element of effeminacy: he is often passive, a plaything of more powerful women, and displays artistic talents – it should be noted that passiveness, the effeminacy suggested by the Venus-like posture, and an artistic spirit are all foregrounded in Cosway's iconic depiction of Kościuszko. The doubled emplotment translates into a generic blend, whereby the more sensational element – imprisonment in *The Spirit* and war in *Thaddeus* – is combined with a domestic romance of the

---

[96] Looser, *Sister Novelists*, ch. 4.
[97] Jane Porter, *The Spirit of the Elbe*, 2 vols (London: T. N. Longman and O. Rees, 1799), vol. 2, p. 18.

nobility's intrigues. In Porter's gothic novel this element takes up most of Volume 2, when a lavish party organised by the Blackenbergs introduces a number of characters of high standing, whose convoluted relationships and intrigues suspend the narrative of terror. At one point, Sigismund – who bears the name of some of Poland's most successful Jagiellonian kings (there is also a housekeeper in the novel named Jagellon) – experiences an attempted seduction by a duchess of Russian origin, taking pride in her acquaintance with Catherine II. 'Fly with me to Russia! and in that glorious country, every transport of love and grandeur shall be yours!', she tempts him.[98] This episode is not the only indication of Porter's likely familiarity with what was happening in Poland at the end of the eighteenth century. Porter would have taken the idea of setting her narrative in Koningstein castle from William Coxe, whose *Travels* features a brief narrative of the imprisonment of King Jan III Sobieski's two sons, James and Constantine (which is Thaddeus of Warsaw's second name, the one he uses in London), in this castle (correctly spelled as Konigstein) in 1704–6. The imprisonment was ordered by Augustus II, who was King of Poland and Saxony at the time, and who decorated Konigstein castle with Poland's national symbols. With these details in mind, the episode of a Russian duchess's unsuccessful seduction of and then revenge against the rightful owner of Koningstein invites an allegorical reading that brings this novel surprisingly close to the subject matter of *Thaddeus of Warsaw*. The publishers Longman and Rees also played a part in reinforcing this thematic correspondence: the first book advertised in the end matter is *The Life of Catherine II. Empress of Russia*.[99]

Porter's account of the fall of Poland in the first volume of *Thaddeus of Warsaw*, including the events surrounding the second and third partitions, is underpinned by gothic frameworks, exploring the adaptability of the female gothic tradition for the purposes of grand historical writing. As Diana Wallace explains, in the hands of women writers the gothic often becomes a tool for making sense of history, a 'kind of metahistory, a way of theorising or producing a philosophy of history'.[100] Porter combines gothic micro-histories with the narrative of the country's ruin, which produces the effect of double-allegorisation: the personal is politicised by way of its entanglement in History, while the macro-narrative of the fall of Poland is personalised through its conceptual proximity to the story of the violated female body. Porter merges the images and metaphors of the imperilled body and the body politic, which is

---

[98] Porter, *The Spirit of the Elbe*, vol. 2, pp. 88–9.
[99] Porter, *The Spirit of the Elbe*, vol. 2, end matter.
[100] Diana Wallace, *Female Gothic Histories: Gender, History and the Gothic* (Cardiff: University of Wales Press, 2013), p. 1.

testimony to her creative use of popular fiction conventions and her recognition of their potential for generic innovation.

The centrality of the gothic framework in the first volume of *Thaddeus* is established by the intertwined and mutually constitutive narratives of the fall of Therese Sobieski and of the fall of Villanow (pol. *Wilanów*), the historical seat of the Sobieski family. The story of Therese's misfortunes is revealed at the beginning of Porter's novel, when Thaddeus is informed of his heritage by his mother. Therese was secretly married and then abandoned by an English visitor to Villanow named Sackville. When it became clear that this Lovelace-like suitor would be unable to fulfil his promises to the pregnant Therese, Thaddeus's grandfather designed and circulated a story that would save the woman's honour and guarantee her son's allegiance with the Sobieski line. When ruined and deserted by her faithless husband, Therese is effectively home-bound, and while Villanow may be a safe haven, of her person as much as her social position, it is also a space of confinement: she considers herself 'immured ... within the Palace of Villanow' (p. 10).[101] The metaphorical imprisonment is also a way of reasserting Therese's identification with the palace, which will be elaborated upon in the war section of the narrative. Thaddeus's father – Sackville – is endowed with a revealing name, suggesting a metaphorical link between ruining Therese and sacking a villa. The guest of Villanow is suggested to be an invader, violating the space of the female body and of the palace, where he was entertained and honoured as a guest. The palace is represented as an embodiment of the ancient magnificence of Poland, so the interpolated tale of Therese Sobieski also foreshadows the misfortunes of Poland, narrated in what follows in the novel. As we have seen, this identification was used before, in *Anzoletta Zadoski*, where the ruinous and thus vulnerable Castle Zadoski becomes a figure of the seduction of Anzoletta perpetrated by Beauchamp, an English visitor to the castle.

The story of the 'sack' of Therese and the metaphorical sack of Villanow perpetrated by Sackville through his violation of the Sobieskis hospitality is doubled by an actual narrative of the sack concluding the Kościuszko Uprising of 1794. The fall of Villanow in Porter's novel is allegorised in three different ways: it is identified with Therese and with feminised Poland, and introduces – as a *villa nova* – a more universal imagery of the New Rome invaded by 'the accumulated hordes of the north' (p. 58), the description given to the Russian 'Goths'. Villanow is idealised in terms of architectural design but also through the enlightened rule imposed by the Sobieski family: the peasants enjoy the

---

[101] References to *Thaddeus* will be parenthetical and use the following edition: Jane Porter, *Thaddeus of Warsaw*, edited by Thomas McLean and Ruth Knezevic (Edinburgh: Edinburgh University Press, 2022).

delights of liberty, unlike in the rest of Poland, and the Masovian Palatinate is effectually an autonomous state organised in accord with the house rules of liberty, tolerance, and hospitality. As such, Porter's representation of Villanow takes her readers back to an idealised vision of the past and suggests her familiarity with the ideas of a '*Gothick* Constitution' and a 'Government of Free-men' as opposed to absolutist monarchy, which was considered to have characterised the flourishing Poland of the past.[102]

In this way, Porter merges two conflicting meanings of 'gothic' in the eighteenth century: she reasserts the civilisation-barbarism divide by staging barbarian Goths sacking the New Rome, but at the same time, she endows the New Rome with the appeal of the positively evaluated 'Gothick' state, an idea she would go on to develop in *The Scottish Chiefs*, with Scotland also conceptualised as an ancient gothic state. This slippage of meaning, or perhaps indented double-voiced discourse, translates itself into how Villanow is represented as an architectural space.

Villanow was erected for King Jan III Sobieski in the late seventeenth century, and its Baroque-classicist design was meant to embody the magnificence of the state during his successful reign (Figure 7). It is briefly described by William Coxe, who also includes a relatively extensive discussion of Sobieski's reign. In Coxe's factual account, little attention is given to the architectural form of the estate, which would have given Porter room for gothic improvisation. As Coxe relates, 'Villanow was built by John Sobieski the conqueror of the Turks and deliverer of Vienna: it was the favourite residence of that great monarch, where he mostly lived when not in arms, and where he closed his days.'[103] Even less information is provided by Stephen Jones's *The History of Poland*, and Porter gives free rein to her gothic imagination in creating a setting that never existed, but which charms with its 'Romantic' appeal. She first establishes the centrality of the estate for her narrative, with the first words of Chapter 1 functioning as a form of mastershot in a manner reminiscent of the opening of *The Mysteries of Udolpho*: 'The large and magnificent palace of Villanow, which stands on the northern bank of the Vistula, was the favourite residence of John Sobieski King of Poland' (p. 7). Porter then constructs her Villanow from two perspectives: that of Thaddeus's attachment and that of Pembroke Somerset as an outsider. To

---

[102] Nick Groom, 'The Term "Gothic" in the Long Eighteenth Century, 1680–1800', in Angela Wright and Dale Townshend (eds), *The Cambridge History of the Gothic. Volume I: Gothic in the Long Eighteenth Century* (Cambridge: Cambridge University Press, 2020), pp. 44–66 (pp. 49–51).

[103] Coxe, *Travels into Poland*, vol. 1, p. 222.

Figure 7 Bernardo Belotto, Wilanów Palace as Seen from the Garden, 1776, The Royal Castle in Warsaw

Thaddeus, as he is leaving his home to take part in the war, Villanow is an enchanted castle, again bringing to mind Radcliffean settings:

> the lofty battlements of Villanow blended with the clouds ... The ivy that mantled over its sides, sparkled with the brightness of a shower which had just fallen; and the rays of the setting sun, gleaming on its shattered wall, made it an object of ... romantic beauty. ... (p. 18)

Somerset, in turn, rationalises his experience. He recognises how, to Thaddeus, the place exudes an aura of enthralment ('You speak so rapturously of your *enchanted castle*, Thaddeus' [p. 41]),[104] but to him – a travelling Englishman – the palace embodies the values of the 'Gothick' past. In a letter to his mother, he wishes to capture 'the real appearance of this palace' and to correct 'the few slight sketches that have been published in England, of Poland' which 'hardly resemble the original' (p. 44). He precedes his account with an extensive description of the picturesque countryside surrounding the palace before offering a vision of Villanow that is not 'real' but constructed, reconciling the poetics and the politics of gothic, and which is not entirely unlike Thaddeus's 'Romantic' perspective:

---

[104] To read on 'enchanted castles' and the gothic tradition, see Dale Townshend, *Gothic Antiquity: History, Romance, and the Architectural Imagination, 1760-1840* (Oxford: Oxford University Press, 2019), pp. 89–130.

> The palace of Villanow, which is castellated, and stands in the midst of a fortress, now burst upon my view. It rears its embattled head from the summit of a hill, that gradually slopes down towards the Vistula, and borders, to the south, the plain of Vola; a spot, so long famous for the election of the kings of Poland. On the north of the building, the earth is cut into natural ramparts, which rise in high succession, till they reach the foundations of the palace, where they terminate, in a noble terrace. These ramparts, covered with grass, overlook the stone-outworks, and spread down to the bottom of the hill, which being cloathed with fine trees and luxuriant underwood, forms such a rich and verdant base to the fortress, as I have not language to describe; were I privileged to be poetical, I would say, that it reminds me of the god of war, sleeping amid roses in the bower of love. Here, the eye may wander over the gifts of bounteous nature arraying hill and dale in all the united treasures of spring and autumn. The forest stretches its yet unsunned arms to the breeze; whilst that breeze comes laden with the fragrance of the tented hay, and the thousand sweets breathed from those flowers which in this delicious country, weep honey.
>
> A magnificent flight of steps led us from the foot of the ramparts up to the gate of the palace. We entered it; and were presently surrounded by a train of attendants, in such sumptuous liveries, that I found myself all at once carried back into the fifteenth century; and might have fancied myself within the courtly halls of our Tudors and Plantagenets. (p. 46)

As mentioned, neither Thaddeus's nor Pembroke's perspective on Villanow gives a sense of what the palace is and was like: built on a plain, in the classical style, with no ivy or other picturesque elements. There is a clear generic agenda behind these sketches: Thaddeus's enthusiastic view of the estate endows it with the enchantment of romance; Pembroke's more detailed and seemingly factual description is still couched in a style that invokes the allure of romance, but combines it with a political message about the villa being a repository of the glorious past. He invokes the Tudors and the Plantagenets here, while elsewhere, when conveying his impressions about the chivalrous noblemen he encountered in Villanow, he relates how they made him think of his 'ancestors' represented in the picture gallery of the Somerset estate. There is a line of ancient 'Gothick' heritage established at this point that unites Pembroke and Thaddeus's backgrounds and foreshadows the romance-like conclusion of the novel where they are revealed to be brothers.

The sketches of Villanow also sustain the conceptual identification of the palace and Therese Sobieski. Thaddeus, when he invites Pembroke, 'was eagerly describing the merits of the Countess and the beauties of his home', we read, declaring that 'Villanow is a perfect paradise; and my mother, the dear angel' (p. 41). The 'angelic' metaphor then translates into Pembroke's account, as he reports on Therese's musical skills, which complement the atmosphere of magnificence with a softening feminine element: 'the Countess sings to us; . . . She has an uncommonly sweet voice, and a taste, which I never heard paralleled . . . whilst the Countess is singing I hardly suffer myself to breathe' (p. 44).

The sack of Villanow culminates the action-packed narrative of the Kościuszko Uprising. After the vivid scenes of the massacre of the Warsaw district of Praga, the Russian 'horde' marches towards Villanow. The sack of the Sobieski estate, which comes to epitomise the fall of Poland, is at the same time the second sack of Therese, whose idealised character makes for an alluring embodiment of feminised Poland as a country. The idea is suggested by the wording Porter uses to account for Thaddeus's perception of the Russian troops, 'busily engaged in sacking the place', as they were moving towards Villanow: 'prowling about, glutted, but not sated with blood . . . and with a ferocity as wanton as unmanly' (p. 80). The elements of bodily horror are endowed with rapist connotations – 'prowling', 'wanton' – and as such, 'This hideous spectacle brought his mother's defenceless state before the eyes of Sobieski' (p. 80). When the spread of total devastation finally reaches Villanow, the narrative zooms in on Thaddeus's final exchange with his mother, and the demolition of the estate coincides with the death of Therese. Porter skilfully captures the simultaneity of the two falls, and she does so using the popular gothic motif of a castle crumbling:

> a sudden volley of fire arms made Thaddeus spring upon his feet. Loud out-cries succeeded. The women rushed into the apartment, screaming, 'The ramparts are stormed!' and the next moment, that quarter of the building rocked to its foundation. The Countess clung to the bosom of her son; Thaddeus clasped her close to his breast, and casting up his petitioning eyes to Heaven, 'O God!' cried he, 'can I not find shelter for my mother!'
> Another burst of cannon was followed by a heavy crash, and the most piercing shrieks, echoed through the palace. 'All is lost!' cried a soldier, who appeared for an instant at the room door, and vanished. (p. 81)

Therese is now literally 'immured' in Villanow, as the Russian demolition doubles Sackville's seduction. The once violated female body is thus deposited in the ruins of the palace, as the identification of the victimised woman and the feminised body politic is made complete.

While the exiled Thaddeus's experiences in London fall beyond this Element's scope of interest, it is significant that, as the protagonist believes he learns more about his father, the link between Sackville and the Russian invaders is reasserted. Thaddeus is informed that his father's misdemeanours in Poland were doubled by his actions towards a London friend, Lady

Tinemouth. Thaddeus consequently calls him a 'barbarian Englishman' (p. 198), and the narrative voice relates his thoughts: 'all [his] filial dreams were blasted by the conviction, that... his mother was the victim of a profligate; that he had sprung from a man who was not merely a villain, but the most wanton, the most despicable of villains' (p. 201). As the novel concludes, it is revealed that there were, in fact, two cousins travelling in Europe, both adopting the false name of Sackville, and that Lady Tinemouth fell victim to the other one. While the resolution partially exonerates Thaddeus's father, at least of the crimes against Lady Tinemouth, the doubling reasserts the parallelism, which is established not only through a conceptual proximity between seduction and sacking a villa, but also by the explicit lexical choices: Sackville is dubbed a 'wanton barbarian', much like the Russian 'horde'.

The London narrative – with Thaddeus's sense of oppression by the nobility and imprisonment for debt in Newgate[105] – also reveals a shadowy presence of a gender reversal gothic narrative familiar not only from the story of Theodore in *The Spirit of the Elbe*, but also from the interpolated tale of the attempted assassination of King Stanislaus narrated by a participant of the events in the earlier section of the novel. This shocking episode is based on a true event that took place in 1771, plotted by the Confederation of Bar, the opposition to the king. It was popularised by William Coxe in his *Travels*, and then Coxe's version was used by Stephen Jones in his *History*. Porter follows Coxe very closely, though embellishes and, indeed, gothicises the language. For example, Coxe's raw: 'The night was exceedingly dark; they were absolutely ignorant of the way; and, as the horses could not keep their legs, they obliged his majesty to follow them on foot, with only one shoe, the other being lost in the dirt',[106] becomes in Porter's version a gothic fairy tale–like narrative:

> The night was now grown so dark, that they could not be sure of their way; and their horses stumbling at every step over stumps of trees and hollows in the earth, encreased their apprehensions to such a degree, that they obliged the king to keep up with them on foot: he literally marked his path with his blood, his shoes having been torn off in the struggle at the carriage. (p. 22)

While the protagonist in Coxe's account is invariably referred to as 'the king' and 'his majesty', preserving the aura of empowerment, Porter brings him closer to the reader and partially deprives him of royal splendour by

---

[105] Thaddeus' reaction on seeing Newgate not only makes sense of the prison in gothic terms but is also reminiscent of his mother's metaphorical and literal immurement in Villanow: 'he beheld the immense walls, within which he believed he should be immured for life, his feet seemed rooted to the ground: and when the massy gates were opened, and closed upon him, he felt as if suddenly deprived of the vital spring of existence' (p. 284).
[106] Coxe, *Travels into Poland*, vol. 1, p. 40.

complementing the conventional addresses with more personalised modes, such as 'Stanislaus', 'the unfortunate Stanislaus' (p. 23), or 'the good Stanislaus' (p. 24). With the assassins in Porter's account consistently dubbed 'banditti', the narrative transforms the assassination plot into a banditti kidnapping narrative, not unlike the familiar episodes in Minerva gothics.

The gothicisation of the kidnapping, and especially Porter's use of the female gothic conventions to tell an anecdote about a male king, underline the broader conceptual approach at play: the story of Poland's fall invites gothic imagery and gothic frameworks; it is a story that dovetails with the prevalent gothic conventions at the time, but which also underlines the more universal, and political, dimensions of the female gothic. Porter draws fascinating lines of identification between endangered bodies – those of Therese and King Stanislaus – and the violated body politic, which may well be read as an elaboration of the metaphor of feminised Poland and her fall, but which also offers alluring and pertinent reflections on the intertwined natures of the personal and the political, and the role of the gothic in addressing these concerns.

3 Catherine Gore's *Polish Tales* (1833): Complicating Poland's Victimhood

Remembered primarily as a widely read author of silver fork novels, Catherine Frances Gore (1798–1861) was a seasoned traveller with historical and political interests, who enjoyed her status as a celebrity author among elitist coteries.[107] Her *Polish Tales* was published by Saunders and Otley in 1833, with a second edition in the same year. This section offers a reading of Gore's *Polish Tales* that shows how the popular form of the tale, as well as the author's explicit indebtedness to Coxe and Porter, enabled her to elaborate upon some of the already recognised aspects of Gothic Poland. Gore's tales offer insights into the appeal of the fallen country in the context of the newly rekindled revolutionary spirit across Europe. The November Uprising against the Russian Empire was the strongest manifestation of this spirit in occupied Poland, and its failure resulted yet again in a heightened interest in the country's tragic fall, not least as

---

[107] Gore's silver fork fiction is discussed, among others, in Edward Copeland, *The Silver Fork Novel: Fashionable Fiction in the Age of Reform* (Cambridge: Cambridge University Press, 2012), and Dianne F. Sadoff, 'The Silver Fork Novel', in John Kucich and Jenny Bourne Taylor (eds), *The Oxford History of the Novel in English: Volume 3: The Nineteenth-Century Novel 1820–1880* (Oxford: Oxford University Press, 2011), pp. 106–21. Both Copeland and Sadoff point to the political turmoil of the 1820s and 1830s, including the spread of popular radicalisms and democratic thinking culminating in the Reform Act of 1832, as the determinative factor in the formation of the silver fork novel. As Sadoff puts it, the silver fork novel 'instructed the middle-class reading public in social virtues and political ideas' (p. 112). Gore's use of the gothic, as will be shown, would have been an alternative way to tackle political concerns.

it was followed by a substantial wave of Polish immigrants arriving in Britain. Gore, as we shall see, was not the only author to use the form of the national tale to respond to the Polish question, but her contribution was the most elaborate, and like Porter in *Thaddeus*, she suggested ways in which this question could be further generalised and allegorised.

In his survey of the novel in the Romantic period, Peter Garside notes that by the 1820s, 'tale' and 'tales' had become more popular title choices than 'novel' and 'romance', and that the popularity of such titles amounted to no less than 34 per cent of all published fiction in the decade.[108] Some of these tales were of a length that is commonly taken to be that of a novel, while others took the form of a short story. This shift in nomenclature probably emerged as a response to Walter Scott's successful *Tales of my Landlord*, the first set of which was published in 1816. As Tim Killick points out, however, consolidating some of the observations made by Garside and earlier by Gary Kelly, 'tale' also held a particular set of associations, such as relating to moral purpose, orality, cross-generational communication, and rural contexts.[109] While initially, Killick continues, 'tales' did not immediately connote 'a specific political or social agenda', in contrast to 'novel' and its 'Jacobin associations',[110] the allure of various national histories as explored through 'tales' opened the political spectrum. The national tale realised 'the Romantic desire to bring together land, history, and nationality',[111] but it was also a channel for expressing relevant political concerns through a poetics of displacement.

Frederic William Naylor Bayley's 1831 *Tales of the Late Revolutions. With A Few Others* opens with a Poland-centred narrative, 'Potoski and Luwarrow; or, The Inmates of Rodzvil', which documents how the national tale in the period established a sense of coherence between the revolutions of the 1790s and the new political situation of the 1820s and early 1830s. The 1830 July revolution in Paris against the Bourbons is simply referred to as 'the French Revolution', and taken to have been an incentive for the Poles, 'the enslaved descendants of Kosiusko [*sic*]', to rebel against the tyranny of Grand Duke Constantine.[112] Bayley's tale is written in the familiar style that combines

---

[108] Peter Garside, James Raven, and Rainer Schöwerling, 'The English Novel in the Romantic Era: Consolidation and Dispersal', in Peter Garside et al., *The English Novel, 1770–1829: A Bibliographical Survey of Prose Fiction Published in the British Isles*, 2 vols (Oxford: Oxford University Press, 2000), 'Table 2. Keywords in Titles, 1800–1829', vol. 2, p. 50.

[109] Tim Killick, *British Short Fiction in the Early Nineteenth Century: The Rise of the Tale* (Aldershot: Ashgate, 2008), pp. 17–18. See also Gary Kelly, *English Fiction of the Romantic Period, 1789–1830* (London and New York: Longman, 1989), pp. 64–5.

[110] Killick, *British Short Fiction in the Early Nineteenth Century*, p. 18.

[111] Killick, *British Short Fiction in the Early Nineteenth Century*, p. 3.

[112] Frederic William Naylor Bayley, *Tales of the Late Revolutions. With A Few Others* (London: Dalton, 1831), p. 46; 8.

historical and gothic modes, though the preface makes clear that the timeframe is contemporary:

> It struck me that the eventful occurrences of the last few months afforded ample scope for such fictions—and that a Romance of Present Times, involving in some degree their spirit and politics, would prove more interesting to you than a Romance of Past History.[113]

The obfuscated sense of immediacy that was created by hastily written Minerva gothics is thus institutionalised as a mode of quasi-political fiction writing, with the brief form of the tale becoming an apt channel for processing and popularising this content.

Apart from establishing a sense of continuity between the two revolutionary decades and the respective generations of freedom fighters – the comrades of 'Kosiusko' are now frail and old but still cherish dreams of liberty and provide support for the young enthusiasts – Bayley's tale situates itself in the longer tradition of fictionalising the Polish cause. A certain degree of readerly competence is required: 'We need not recur to the past history of Poland, in order to trace the events that have led to the present crisis. The occurrences of the last century are still fresh in the minds of our readers'.[114] The same might be said of the gothic fictions inspired by these events, and Bayley would have expected his readers to identify the literary allusions, too. Recycling the stories of exile and disenfranchisement familiar from *Anzoletta Zadoski* and *Radzivil*, 'Potoski and Luwarrow' features Count Zudofski, who fought in the Kościuszko Uprising and, in its aftermath, was dispossessed of his seat – the Castle of Rodzvil. He retired to the country and started a new life in seclusion, accompanied by his daughters, in a place now called Rodzvil Cottage. When the right time comes, Rodzvil Cottage is where enthusiastic Potoski finds his love and fuel for his revolutionary ideas, both of which are brutally restrained by his false friend Luwarrow. The story concludes with the two Zudofski sisters escaping the scene of murder and Luwarrow receiving justice from the hands of the revolutionaries as the November Uprising breaks out on 29 November 1830. In closing the tale Bayley expresses hopes that the revolution will ultimately prove to be successful; it did not, and instead provided further incentive to lament the country, much like the Poland of the 1790s, in a manner that could well follow the vein of the Romantic verse sung by Potoski as he takes a boat across the Vistula towards Rodzvil Cottage:

---

[113] Bayley, *Tales of the Late Revolutions*, p. v.
[114] Bayley, *Tales of the Late Revolutions*, p. 5. The eponymous names of Potoski and Luwarrow would be intended to echo Ignacy Potocki, one of the military leaders of the Kościuszko Uprising, and General Alexander Suvorov, responsible for the massacre of Praga.

> Our poor country—snakes enfold her,
> Fair and lovely though she be,
> And unpitying kings behold her,
> Now no longer great and free![115]

Published two years after Bayley's collection, Gore's *Polish Tales* appeared when memories of the revolutionary failure were still fresh, and as Polish immigrants were making themselves at home in London and other major British cities. Gore's tales would have been designed as introductions to aspects of Polish history particularly relevant for the new coteries committed to the Polish cause who gathered around Polish exiles, such as the Literary Association of the Friends of Poland established in 1832 by Thomas Campbell, the poet known for 'The Fall of Poland' and its famous concluding line: 'And Freedom shrieked, as Kosciusko fell!'[116] The constitution of the Association defined it as 'instituted for the general knowledge of the history and events of the ancient kingdom of Poland and for collecting all such information as may tend to preserve in the public mind of Great Britain a lively interest in the condition of that country'.[117] Branches of the organisation were established across Britain, and the famous Polish immigrants Adam Jerzy Czartoryski and Julian Ursyn Niemcewicz, both endowed with political as well as literary talents, 'soon became lions in London society'.[118] Another notable Polish exile at this time, Stanisław Koźmian, later a translator of Shakespeare, recalls of one such meeting in early 1833:

> Around nine o'clock in the evening, I was conducted to the assembly. The room was nearly full when I arrived. An English gentleman had already begun reading a dissertation on the partitions of Poland. Following this, another person recited poetry, which was interrupted with frequent and enthusiastic applause. Finally, the violinist Maciejowski performed several patriotic melodies. Once this concluded, small circles were formed, and animated discussions ensued regarding subjects pertinent to the purpose of the gathering. Some engaged in disputes concerning historical events, others put forward proposals – all were united by one common thought and objective. There were a dozen or so women present. Of these, I recall but one. She was of modest height, rather plump, though still quite youthful. I was informed that this was the renowned author Mrs. Gore, who had recently undertaken the writing of Polish tales. It was also said that among those present were Lady Morgan and Miss Porter, the celebrated author of the famous romance *Thaddeus of Warsaw*, but these ladies had already taken their

---

[115] Bayley, *Tales of the Late Revolutions*, p. 20.
[116] Thomas Campbell, *The Pleasures of Hope and Other Poems* (Edinburgh: Mundell & Son; and Longman & Rees, and J. Wright, 1795), p. 30.
[117] Quoted after Gleason, *The Genesis of Russophobia in Great Britain*, p. 120.
[118] Gleason, *The Genesis of Russophobia in Great Britain*, p. 121.

leave before I had the opportunity to inquire about the identities of those still in attendance.[119]

Lady Morgan's first published piece after the meeting was a short closet drama curiously titled 'Manor Sackville' (in *Dramatic Scenes from Real Life*, 1833), which was concerned with riots in Ireland. As we shall see, Gore's tales also thematise social unrest, while the potential allusion to Porter's incredibly popular *Thaddeus*, which is also explicitly referred to in Gore's *Polish Tales*, puts these three women writers in creative conversation around the major political events, social phenomena and national struggles of Ireland, Scotland, and Poland.

The instructively entertaining appeal of the tales, which (incidentally) were published shortly after Gore's *Hungarian Tales*, doubtless provoked by the emerging nationalist thought and reforms in the 1820s and early 1830s in that country, was praised by an anonymous reviewer for *The Spectator*:

> IF Mrs. GORE had no other quality but her facility, she would rank among the wonders of the existing literary world. Her execution keeps pace with conception: she is at home in most parts of Europe; and wherever she places her scene, takes up the manners of the people as if she had been born and bred among them. Then she has no sooner transported our imaginations to the Vistula or the Danube, the Alps or the Krapaks, than all of a sudden, with a conjuror's rapidity, we find her seated in the centre of London fashion, or at home in all the routine of a country gentleman's house, as if she had never had another thought than just catching the folly of the hour, the foible of the season.[120]

---

[119] 'Około dziewiątéj wieczorem zaprowadzono mię na owo zebranie. Salę zastałem prawie pełną. Jakiś Anglik czytał najprzód rozprawę o rozbiorach Polski. Następnie, ktoś inny deklamował poezyą, przerywaną rzęsistemi oklaskami. W końcu skrzypek Maciejowski odegrał kilka melodyi ojczystych. Gdy to przeszło, potworzyły się kółka żwawo rozprawiających o przedmiotach tyczących się celu zgromadzenia. Jedni się spierali o jakieś wypadki historyczne, inni podawali projekta, wszystkich ożywiała jedna myśl i cel jeden. Dam było kilkanaście. Z tych jedną tylko pamiętam. Była to niska i pękata ale dość jeszcze młoda osoba. Powiedziano mi że to sławna autorka Pani Gore, która się właśnie zajmowała pisaniem powieści polskich. Podobno były w tém zgromadzeniu i Lady Morgan i Panna Porter, autorka słynnego romansu *Tadeusz z Warszawy*, ale te wyszły za nim zacząłem się o przytomne osoby rozpytywać.' Stanisław Koźmian, *Anglia i Polska* (Poznań: Nakładem Księgarni Jana Konstantego Żupańskiego, 1862), pp. 11–12. Translation mine. Interestingly, the chronology of Gore's life, as sketched in Winifred Hughes' ODNB entry and in Andrea Hibbard and Edward Copeland's edition of *Cecil*, sees her move to Paris along with her husband in 1832. Koźmian's retrospective writing might have been inaccurate in terms of chronology, or, alternatively, Gore might have joined her husband slightly later. See Winifred Hughes, 'Gore [née Moody], Catherine Grace Frances (1798–1861), *Oxford Dictionary of National Biography Online*, https://doi.org/10.1093/ref:odnb/11091; Catherine Gore, *Cecil: or, The Adventures of a Coxcomb (1841)*, edited by Andrea Hibbard and Edward Copeland, *Silver Fork Novels, 1826–1841*, vol. 6 (London: Pickering & Chatto, 2005).

[120] *The Spectator* 246 (1833): 236.

The reviewer values Gore's faithful recreation of her changing settings; her cosmopolitan 'homeliness' everywhere rather than, we could add, gothic displacement and obfuscation. Her writing method and style are appreciated further on in the review: the book is considered not to 'bear any marks of haste or rapid composition' despite being written in connection with the immediate political context and 'the state of feeling in this country towards Poland'. Gore is credited with the possession of a thorough knowledge of Polish manners and history, her writing endowed with 'truth and force' and embellished with 'high value' pictures of scenery. The review gives a good sense of the divide separating the Italianate Minerva renditions of Poland from the more informed but perhaps less attractive – at least in terms of immersive reading – settings recreated by Gore.

In 1833 Gore had not yet written her best-known silver fork novels, such as *Cecil; or, the Adventures of a Coxcomb* (1841), and would still have remained indebted to earlier traditions of writing, including gothic and historical fiction, displaying her competence in adapting 'the most recent literary trends of the transitional early nineteenth century in order to maintain her popularity as the century progressed', as Samantha Belcher aptly summarises.[121] Gore's *Theresa Marchmont; or, The Maid of Honour* is a well-written gothic tale published in 1824. It belongs to a tradition that has been termed 'Bluebeard gothic':[122] a 'mad' wife imprisoned for life in a detached mansion; her 'melancholic' husband remarrying; a bedroom haunting experienced by the new wife; the explained supernatural that reveals the secret; a resolution that turns the new wife into a 'maid of honour' in a selfless act of female solidarity. *Theresa Marchmont* confirms Gore's investment in female gothic conventions and provides an illuminating context, as will be shown, for one of her Polish tales, as well as being a likely model for Charlotte Brontë's *Jane Eyre*, along with other narratives of the period that explore the haunting presence of 'mad' women and bigamous marriage plots.[123] Gore's other earlier fictions include

---

[121] Samantha Lee Belcher, '"A most vexatious trade to make bread by": The Authorial Careers of Christian Isobel Johnstone and Catherine Gore, 1824–1846' (PhD diss., Durham University 2021), p. 80.

[122] Heta Pyrhönen, *Bluebeard Gothic: Jane Eyre and Its Progeny* (Toronto: University of Toronto Press, 2010).

[123] For further reading on Gore and the Brontës, see Belcher, 'A most vexatious trade to make bread by', pp. 121–9. Maia McAleavey, in *The Bigamy Plot: Sensation and Convention in the Victorian Novel* (Cambridge: Cambridge University Press, 2015), does not comment on Gore's earlier narratives, but offers a competent overview of how popular the pattern would become. Gore's work is likewise absent from the classic discussions of 'mad' women in nineteenth-century fiction: Elaine Showalter, *The Female Malady: Women, Madness, and English Culture, 1830-1980* (Harmondsworth: Penguin, 1985); and Sandra M. Gilbert and Susan Gubar, *The Madwoman in the Attic: The Woman Writer and the Nineteenth-Century Literary Imagination* (New Haven and London: Yale University Press, 1984). Deborah Weiss

the two-tale volume *The Lettre de Cachet; A Tale. The Reign of Terror; A Tale* (1827). Using a narrative framework that capitalises on the popularity of historical writing in the 1820s – moving from the times of Louis XIV to the French Revolution – the tales further ponder systems of abuse against women, the embodiment of which in the two tales are scheming aristocrats.

The eponymous *lettre de cachet* of the first narrative was an inherently gothic institution in pre-Revolutionary France, whereby through a sealed letter the monarch could sentence anyone to prison, exile, or confinement without any legal substantiation. Using the letter for the title of the tale thus effectively doubles up on the title of the following story, while the actual narrative recycles themes familiar from *Theresa Marchmont*: an imprisoned woman who goes 'mad' and a 'melancholic' aristocrat who bigamously marries again upon his monstrous mother's arranged confinement of the first wife through the titular *lettre du cachet*. The female gothic framework depends on the allegorisation of the eponymous letter, which stands for broader networks of oppression. *The Reign of Terror* can be interpreted in a similar manner, in as much as the actual representation of the Revolution, 'the maniacal fury of an excited mob',[124] becomes a mere background to the more tangible terror experienced by innocent Estella from the aristocratic intrigues against her. The appeal of historical fiction writing and the contexts of grand politics are used with a generalist agenda in both stories to offer tales of women's imprisonment. Gore's method aligns with what Jane Porter had defined as a combination of 'facts of real history or biography' with the 'illustrative machinery of the imagination', and there is a clear political purpose to her fictional machinery.[125]

Gore's three-volume *Polish Tales* is effectively a set of three independent titles: a novel-length narrative, *The Confederates of Lubionki* (Volumes 1 and 2); a shorter, though still substantial story, *The Mill of Mariemont; or The Fortunes of Stanislas* (Volumes 2 and 3); and a short fiction entitled 'The Pasieka, or Bee Farm', which closes Volume 3. Gore appended explanatory notes to the collection, providing her readers with further contextual and historical information. These notes also situate Gore's narratives in the network of previous writings on Poland, in particular Coxe's *Travels* and Porter's *Thaddeus*, to which she explicitly refers. The tales can well be read as standalone narratives, but they are nevertheless arranged chronologically. The first

---

has recently provided more insight into 'mad' women preceding Bertha Mason and covered the work of lesser-known women writers of the Romantic period. Gore, however, is similarly absent from this discussion. Deborah Weiss, *Women and Madness in the Early Romantic Novel: Injured Minds, Ruined Lives* (Manchester: Manchester University Press, 2024).

[124] Catherine Gore, *The Lettre de Cachet; A Tale. The Reign of Terror; A Tale* (London: J. Andrews, 1827), p. 344.

[125] Porter, *Thaddeus of Warsaw*, 1831, p. vi.

story is set at the twilight of Augustus III's reign, when courtly extravagances, political factions and external pressures reduced Poland to being a weak and vulnerable country, driven by general dissatisfaction. The eponymous confederates form a clandestine organisation that includes representatives of such diverse backgrounds as the landed gentry, enslaved peasants, members of the Jewish community, and local Jesuits. They fight for the abolition of serfdom, inspired by the liberal ideas promoted, rather surprisingly, by their Jesuit leader. The tale concludes on the eve of the royal election, at which point the subsequent narrative takes its turn.

The title of *The Mill of Mariemont* might suggest a story of the attempted assassination of King Stanislas, with the eponymous mill being, as we remember from Coxe's and Porter's versions, the setting for the happy conclusion of the treacherous plot. In fact, Gore presents us with a fully fledged piece of historical fiction, telling Stanislas's story from his travels, education (organised by Charles Hanbury Williams), and his diplomatic mission to Russia – which includes an account of his romance with Catherine shortly before she seized power – to his election as King of Poland, secured by the new empress, and the events that ensue. The sensational story of the kidnapping takes no more than a quarter of the whole tale and unfolds in the second part, preceded by a vivid account of Stanislas's reign à la mode. Finally, 'Pasieka; or, Bee farm' is set after Stanislas's reign, in the aftermath of the partitions, against the historical backdrop of the unrest in Vilnius involving progressive students who opposed the imperial authorities.

The three tales are invariably romance narratives, staging the divide between the old and the new. Gore avails herself of the typical structures of emplotment, such as love triangles and quadruples, the conflicts between generations and representatives of different social standing, between individuals and authorities, and the clash of micro- and macrohistories. In each tale authority is opposed, which is understandable in the revolutionary context of publication and the implied reading audiences, although the narrative voice wavers in its sympathy towards rebels and conspirators. The confederates are represented in an ambiguous manner, which underlines both their uncivilised savagery and the justness of their liberal claims. Stanislas's unsuccessful assassins are villains, but not necessarily without a cause, given the background of the king's hedonistic and largely passive reign. It is only the Vilnius opposition in 'Pasieka' that is unequivocally heroic. This ambivalent approach to the revolutionary cause is also visible in *The Reign of Terror*, where the aristocratic class is depicted as deserving little less than the rebels' ferocity, and yet the Parisian 'mob' is represented en masse as a destructive force that attracts little narrative sympathy.

As for *Polish Tales*, there would have been specific contextual reasons for this conflicted perspective given the background of Gore's potential readers in pro-Polish coteries: they were advocates of freedom, but would not necessarily support a class revolution against the nobility; they would have remembered Stanisław August's faults and vices alongside his accomplishments, and the memories of anti-Russian resistance, not only during the November Uprising but also in the early 1820s at Vilnius University, were still fresh. That Gore was writing to the moment, and with her potential readers in mind, is made clear in the appendix. While the members of the Czartoryski family are not presented in the best of lights in the first two tales – they are scheming and overly ambitious – Gore's note explains that these sentiments should not be read as targeted at Prince Adam Jerzy Czartoryski, who was involved in the November Uprising and then in the London coteries: 'The present Prince, a man commanding the universal respect of his countrymen, has sacrificed immense possessions to the liberality of his political opinions; ... the list of living Polish patriots contains no name more eminent than that of Czartoryski'.[126]

The three narratives reveal a gothic, especially Radcliffean, provenance in terms of structure and characterisation, with stock tropes such as epigraphs (with sources ranging from Petrarch to Byron), interpolated poems, landscape descriptions, secret subterranean passages, banditti, despotic fathers, scheming monks, enthusiastic lovers, and musically inclined heroines. The tale mostly indebted to the gothic tradition is *The Confederates*, while the other two stories explore the gothic potential to a more limited degree. But even in *The Confederates* the immersive and suspenseful qualities of the gothic are compromised by attempts at contextual verisimilitude: tedious historical remarks, annotations, and the numerous Polish-language embellishments. The latter would have been particularly alienating to Gore's English readers, as she herself acknowledges in the preface to the second edition, writing that they 'afforded grounds of disapproval to many English readers'.[127] Gore's take on Poland and its potential as a gothic setting reconciles Porter's attempts at historical accuracy with Minerva's absorption of new spatial possibilities into its formal gothic machinery. The final product may lack Minerva's page-turning charm, but retains *Thaddeus*'s conceptual advancement, whereby a gothic framework elucidates the wrongs of history; in Gore's case, the emphasis is moved to class inequalities and serfdom. Gore's narratives

---

[126] Catherine Gore, *Polish Tales*, 3 vols (London: Saunders and Otley, 1833), vol. 3, p. 318. Further references to Gore's tales are parenthetical.

[127] Bayley in 'Potocki and Luwarrow' admits to his doubts about the naming of the two female characters: 'As we are, however, convinced that their fair names would be utterly unpronounceable to the English tongues, we must beg permission to substitute others in their stead, which we pledge ourselves will be equally romantic, and not half as difficult. What think ye of Lolia and Pulchrine?', *Tales of the Late Revolutions*, p. 26.

came out at the twilight of the early gothic, when its formal identity as a literary genre gradually disintegrated and evolved into a mode that would be readily activated in various types of narrative fiction. Gore's form of the 'national story', as she labelled it, is one such formal context, and while the numerous occasions when the gothic mode is switched on do not make the tales generically gothic, they do provide insight into the foregrounded elements of the Polish setting and history that were deemed appropriate to trigger the mode.

The first two narratives by Gore can be read as writing back to Porter by way of building on underdeveloped episodes: the enfranchisement of the peasants and anti-royal conspiracies, including the attempted assassination of King Stanisław. *The Confederates of Lubionki* elaborates on Coxe's discussion of anti-royal confederations on the eve of the partitions and on Porter's idyllic vision of enfranchised serfs in the Masovian Palatinate. Gore's narrative merges these two topics to showcase the political tensions of the time: a confederation of revolutionary freedom fighters opposes both institutional serfdom in Poland and the Russian sympathies of some members of the nobility, such as the Czartoryskis, while the growing dissatisfaction with fictional Count Czelenszki's enlightened rule in Wodarko, Masovia, and his overturning of a centuries-long feudal system raises awareness of the broader history of labour exploitation in the country. Against this background of historical turmoil and conflicted policies of the old and the new, Mineczka (a Radcliffean heroine), Doska (the abused daughter of a peasant), Juliusz Felinski (a Byronic freedom fighter), and Konstanty Felinski (a foppish officer of the Czartoryski camp) are entangled in a romantic quadruple and struggle with their diverse backgrounds, political factions, and despotic fathers.

In addressing the question of what was often considered as institutional slavery in Poland,[128] Gore corrects the idyllic vision of Villanow as a seat of liberty by offering better-informed insights into the issues of enfranchisement and serfdom. Her equivalent of Porter's idealised Masovian Palatine, Count

---

[128] Cf. *The Calumet* devoted to 'The Downfall of Poland': 'Both Greece and Poland have been nations of heroes and slaves from time immemorial. They oppressed others, and have in turn been oppressed. They both have had domestic slaves, over whom they have tyranized more than their conquerors have tyranized over them ... It is a little remarkable, that those nations which have been the most warlike, have generally had the most slavery, either personal or political, and it seems but a righteous retribution of providence that those who had others in slaver, should themselves, in turn, be slaves.' *The Calumet* 1:9 (1832): 260. On the other hand, British political discourse was able to see the differences between slavery and serfdom. For example, the parliamentary debate on 9 July 1833 devoted to the 'Affairs of Poland' sees Mr Thomas Atwood argue: 'It was customary in England to speak of Poland as a land of slaves. But it was a great mistake to suppose that slavery was common in Poland. That kingdom had never been reduced to slavery. There was no word in the language to express "slave"; they had no nearer approach to it than the words expressing "prisoner of war". It was only from choice the serf was attached to the soil—not from the operation of slavery.' *Hansard*. House of Commons, 9 July 1833, vol. 19, p. 416.

Czelenski is considered a quixotic free-thinker, whose enlightened reforms are opposed by his neighbours as foreign imports that go against Poland's 'ancient constitution' (vol. 1, p. 9). The confederates, being an assembly of revolutionaries who come from various classes, are accordingly regarded by the dissatisfied Szlachta as 'plotters of evil who would violate the ancient charters of our free constitution' (vol. 1, p. 141). Gore thus provides a broader panorama of Poland's convoluted relationship with 'freedom', whereby the landed gentry's unrestrained liberties in terms of their governability by central authorities were at the same time sanctioning a centuries-long history of institutional serfdom in the country. Poland's ancient constitution, in Gore's narrative, is not 'Gothick' in the Whiggish sense, as Porter's vision of Villanow had implied. It is gothic because it legitimates monstrous oppressors who exploit the serfs, as one of the confederates vividly puts it:

> —Ye,—ye, the oppressors,—the scourgers,—the smiters with the sword,—ye who make laws that grind the very bones of the children of the land; ye, who live in pampered sloth, that the life-sickened boor may drag on his weary days, with scarce of bread or sleep to brace his muscles for his task, —ye, who by force of gold and numbers, suck out our strength like vampires, and trample on the exhausted carcase;—ye, who mangle our sons with your Batogs, who bring our daughters to shame, and dishonour the grey hairs of their mothers—. . . —ye will be the first to perish. (vol. 1, pp. 201–2)

Gore deploys the flourishing trope of aristocratic vampirism, memorably conceptualised in John Polidori's *The Vampyre* (1819), to indicate that Poland in the late eighteenth century was not Porter's innocent damsel but a country participating in systemic class abuse. This had already been noted by John Thelwall, in whose abolitionist *The Daughter of Adoption* (1801) we read that 'slavery still maintains its ground in Poland, in Turkey, and in Russia'.[129] Writing about the ways in which nineteenth-century gothic reflected the 'immediate repercussions' of transatlantic slavery, Maisha Wester points to how it obfuscated the boundaries between the villain and the victim, pondering 'the question of responsibility for the chaos and violence arising from slavery and its inevitable insurrections'.[130] Wester's focus concerns echoes of colonial unrest embodied through racially othered characters, but her point is also relevant to Gore's representation of the turmoil in Poland, where the imperilled, feminised state

---

[129] John Thelwall, *The Daughter of Adoption*, 4 vols (London: R. Phillips, 1801), vol. 2, p. 7.
[130] Maisha Wester, 'Nineteenth-Century British and American Gothic and the History of Slavery', in Dale Townshend and Angela Wright (eds), *The Cambridge History of the Gothic. Volume II: Gothic in the Nineteenth Century* (Cambridge: Cambridge University Press, 2020), pp. 394–415 (pp. 414–15).

facing imperial terror is also seen to be part of the problem in the wider system of institutionalised class inequalities. Indeed, one of the confederates dismisses the accusation that they are starting a revolution when the country is in danger by saying:

> Had she proved a tender and a nursing mother alike to all her children, ... no foreign enemy would have prevailed against her ... Animated by that one proud gathering-word of 'POLSKA!'—the people,—they who dig her soil and water it with the sweat of their brows and the tears of their wretchedness,—they—even they—would have joined hand in hand, and formed a frontier of iron around her provinces. (vol. 1, pp. 203–4)

Gore's approach to Poland echoes Porter's in as much as both authors use a gothic framework to address the question of Poland's 'ancient constitution', although they would have had divergent aims in their representations. Written at the height of the 'Kościuszko craze', Porter's *Thaddeus* followed the partitions almost immediately, when the possibility of Britain's involvement in the Polish cause was still on the table. Gore's tale was written after several decades of Poland's non-existence as a free state, after a substantial wave of emigration to Britain, when it had already become apparent that the political interests, and allies, of Poland and Britain were not to be reconciled. Gore lacks Porter's enthusiasm and problematises Poland's role in European structures of abuse and oppression.

While Gore takes her task seriously, an earlier comic tale included in Marion and Margaret Corbett's *Tales and Legends* (1828) adopts a light-hearted, satirical mode to ridicule stereotypical flaws of the Polish nobility; as such, it merits acknowledgement as a likely point of reference for Gore. 'Count Borworjarginski: A Polish Tale' features the eponymous count and his faithful steward Pontosky, their names alluding to two personages who would have been familiar to an English audience: the celebrated 'dwarf', Count Boruwlaski, and King Poniatowski. The generic names are suggestive of cultural stereotyping, and indeed the tale, which in terms of plot revolves around generational conflicts regarding inheritance and marriage, offers a larger-than-life image of a Polish nobleman who arranges for the tips of his fingers to be cut off as a counter-gambling procedure and risks losing all his teeth as an absurdly severe punishment for gluttony over the Lent period. He is rash, headstrong, modestly gifted in terms of intellect, and enjoys showing off his traditional garb. His family quarrels lead to 'a state of rebellion' at home, with one suitor 'taking a ball in his leg' and the other one suffering 'the loss of an eye'.[131] The tale is

---

[131] Marion and Margaret Corbett, 'Count Borwojarginski: A Polish Tale', in *Tales and Legends*, 3 vols (Edinburgh: Cadell; London: Simpkin and Marshall, 1828), vol. 2, pp. 233–96 (p. 277).

a concise piece of ridicule, at the same time indicating an inherently gothic potential of the subject matter. The tale begins conventionally: 'THE bell of the great Minster in Warsaw had just tolled twelve, when the domestics of Count Borworjarginski were suddenly aroused from their slumbers, by thundering blows at the gate of the palace'.[132] What follows is an exercise in bodily grotesque, as the count makes sure he would no longer be enslaved to gambling, and then the narrative centres on Borworjarginski's indomitable attempts at making sure his niece, who is under his care, marries according to his wishes. Essentially a tale involving a wicked uncle and a persecuted niece, with hints at the threat of women's rebellion at home, set in a Catholic country that pulls out the teeth of those who eat too much over Lent, 'Count Borworjarginski' reroutes the gothic towards satire; but it also provides a meaningful context for Gore's ambivalent view of Poland, cured of the 'Kościuszko craze' fascination as exemplified by Jane Porter.

This difference is perhaps best visible in Gore's second tale, *The Mill of Mariemont*, which was inspired by Porter and offers an extended prequel to an episode of *Thaddeus of Warsaw*: the kidnapping of the king. The historical events here are underpinned by romance emplotment, with Stanislas's 'fortunes' driven by his involvement in a love triangle, where Catherine II performs the role of an abandoned mistress who takes revenge on Stanislas and his beloved Axinia, whom he met in Oranienbaum and with whom he subsequently renewed his acquaintance on her arrival in Poland. Stanislas wavers between the roles of being Catherine's puppet, a cynical Casanova who expects political gain from his affair with the future empress, and that of a romantic, passionate youth who promises to change his rakish life and rectify his political negligence when he is already a monarch for the sake of heroic Axinia. Catherine is depicted as a conventionally 'hysterical' lover, monster, and ruthless tyrant, with the fall of Poland presented as resulting from the revengeful passions of a humiliated lover. Gore does not explore the gothic potential of the narrative of kidnapping, even if she retains the banditti references and Stanislas's passivity as 'an effeminate and wounded King' (vol. 3, p. 201). The treacherous plot, and its foregrounded role in the title, was meant to attract a readership, but the central aspect of the tale is Stanislas's evolution as king. His growth is depicted as prompted by fictitious Axinia's repeated entreaties, urging him to usher in just and enlightened reforms, including those of equality and freedom for all. As such, Stanislas's fictionalised evolution would match the broader programme realised by Gore, which, according to Copeland, was to 'teach her young aristocrats ... about political and social changes'.[133]

---

[132] Corbett, 'Count Borworjarginski', p. 235.   [133] Copeland, *The Silver Fork Novel*, p. 167.

Gore thus reinforces the abolitionist message of the previous tale only to complicate it in the third one. 'Pasieka' includes a cautionary narrative told by an old nurse, whose marriage with a representative of a lower class brought life-long misery. Reminiscent of similar warnings about racial intermarriage, the nurse's story shows how her peasant spouse's disease – *Plica Polonica* (Polish plait) – which he had also inherited, was passed onto their offspring, killing them all one by one. The nurse now warns her charge Dzidzilia against Ludwyk, a newcomer to the bee farm, pointing to the scars on the head as indicators of the *Plica*. In the resolution it transpires that the scars were incurred in Ludwyk's struggle against the tsarist authorities in Vilnius, and the patriot hero is gladly accepted as a new family member. What this happy ending glosses over is the uncomfortable association of the *Plica* with the peasants, which is grounded in the stereotypes of exoticised and racialised Poles that circulated at the time. Coxe's *Travels into Poland* contains a vivid presentation of the disease:

> the *Plica Polonica* is supposed to proceed from an acrid viscous humour penetrating into the hair, which is tubular: it then exudes either from its sides or extremities, and clots the whole together, either in separate folds, or in one undistinguished mass. Its symptoms, more or less violent, ... are itchings, swellings, eruptions, ulcers, intermitting fevers, pains in the head, languor, lowness of spirits, rheumatism, gout, and, sometimes even convulsions, palsy, and madness.[134]

Coxe concludes that 'This disorder is thought hereditary; and is proved to be contagious when in a virulent state', and then gives a list of the purported reasons that underline the racial politics at play: 'the Polish air', 'unwholesome water', and 'the gross inattention of the natives to cleanliness'.[135] In fact, *Plica Polonica* was not caused by a disease, but was an unhealthy, and admittedly grotesque, form of hairstyle that evolved at the crossover of fashion and superstition. As Larry Wolff explains, it was weaponised by Enlightenment thinkers to spread stereotypes about Eastern Europeans and their barbaric ancestry in a manner similar to how *Plica Judaica* was used in antisemitic discourse.[136] The false belief that it was caused by a contagious disease continued to spread in the Victorian period, despite growing medical knowledge. In Gore's tale it becomes an indicator of racial difference that is used to reinforce class divisions in a manner that contradicts the egalitarian discourse of *The Confederates*. In the context of Polish emigration in the 1830s, Gore's reference to the *Plica* contagion risks going beyond its original context of class distinctions and turning into a disturbing nationalist *ressentiment*.

---

[134] Coxe, *Travels into Poland*, vol. 1, pp. 280–1. [135] Coxe, *Travels into Poland*, vol. 1, p. 282.
[136] Wolff, *Inventing Eastern Europe*, pp. 29–31.

Figure 8 Eglise et Couvent de Czenstochowa, Leonard Chodźko, La Pologne, historique, litteraire, monumentale et illustree (Paris: Leclerc, 1835–42), Śląska Biblioteka Cyfrowa.

Like Porter in her imaginative depiction of the palace of Villanow, and as with the Minerva fictions, Gore also elaborates on specific aspects of the Polish setting that proved particularly attractive and relevant for the gothic mode. In the curtailed narrative of Stanislas's kidnapping, Gore decided not to explore the spatial possibilities offered by moonlit action in the country, giving a tinge of Radcliffean aesthetics only to the brief depiction of the Jasna Góra monastery in Częstochowa (though closer to reality than Porter's rendering of the Sobieski estate, see Figure 8), where Stanislas was meant to have been imprisoned and executed:

> The fortress of Czenstochowa selected for his reception, was a place that in itself suggested projects of violence.—Situated in a gorge of the mountains that separate Poland from Moravia among hoary forests and desolate solitudes, there was little probability that the unfortunate monarch should escape the vindictive hands of those so eagerly intent on his extermination. (vol. 3, p. 165)

In 'Pasieka', Samogitia is the seat of heathen superstition, although the fear that Ludwyk's killing of a 'sacred snake' would activate a curse is to be taken with a pinch of salt, merely as a further illustration of 'the purity and simplicity of the antique time' that Samogitians have managed to preserve (vol. 3, p. 248). A fully fledged gothic setting is deployed in Gore's first tale.

From the very beginning of *The Confederates*, it is clear that Poland is not rich in stereotypically mountainous gothic sceneries. The epigraph opening the tale suggests that 'inhabitants of extensive plains' are more likely to fall under absolute rule. And while the Italianate Minerva fictions gave the impression that all of Poland was characterised by rocky Carpathian mountains, their caves, mines, and underground passages, Gore respects the actual realities and gothicises them in her own way: what the Mines of Wieliczka offered Lathy, the Polish ancient forests give to Gore. While the central role of the Forest of Death in *De Willenberg* depended on allegorisation and generalisation, Gore's forest is particularised, in a manner reminiscent of Lathy's mines. The Forest of Lubloyst 'embosoms' the titular Lubionki, and Gore tends to refer to it using the Polish word *Puszcza*. In the explanatory notes, Gore explains that '"*Puszcza*" ... is very inadequately expressed by "Forest," which conveys to an English mind the impression of the glades of Windsor or the New Forest, instead of the *wilderness* or *uncultivated lands* implied by the Polish word Puszcza' (vol. 3, pp. 322–3). Gore was probably inspired by what she would have read and heard about the ancient Białowieża Forest (pol. *Puszcza Białowieska*), north-east of Masovia in the Polish-Lithuanian borderland, which was also a backdrop to revolutionary action in 1831 and hosted banditti-like guerrilla troops (Figure 9).[137]

An extensive description of this forest was published in Warsaw in 1826 as *Mémoire descriptif sur la forêt impériale de Białowieza en Lithuanie* by Juliusz Brincken, excerpts from which were published in English in *The Edinburgh New Philosophical Journal* for July–October 1830. Amidst rich factual information, the excerpts include observations that can also be discerned from Gore's representation, such as those concerned with the hamlets in the forest, with their wood cottages and 'wild' inhabitants ('as unpretending as the dwellings, and as rude and uncultivated as the surrounding wilds'), and the impenetrability of the woods. The *Puszcza* is Europe's dark spot; as we read, 'European culture and rational forestry have had no influence on this forest', and its 'heart of darkness' is the '*Unknown region*' (spelled as '*Niezeanow*', likely referring to the reservoir Nieznanowo), 'rendered quite impassable from the multitude of trunks of trees rooted up and crossing one another in all directions'.[138] Gore further gothicises the forest: the *Puszcza* has its mysteries and demons; one

---

[137] Tomasz Samojlik, Anastasia Fedotova, Piotr Daszkiewicz, and Ian D. Rotherham, *Białowieża Primeval Forest: Nature and Culture in the Nineteenth Century* (Cham: Springer, 2020), pp. 62–3.

[138] *The Edinburgh New Philosophical Journal* 9 (1830): 289–90.

Figure 9 Jan Lewicki, The Inhabitants of the Forest of Bialowieza, Les costumes du peuple Polonais (Paris: Librairie Polonaise, 1841), The National Museum in Kraków

can marvel at its picturesque beauty, get lost, and experience delight and terror alike; it produces sounds deemed supernatural, likely coming from the Lady of the Forest who haunts it. Gore also underlines the labyrinthine quality of the *Puszcza*, whereby one's chances of finding or losing the way depend on the ability to read the forest: to identify the right log, ancient tree, or barely discernible path.

The *Puszcza* setting is linked to the larger gothic framework by hosting the rebels in their leader Xavery's cottage, 'in the depth of the forest' (vol. 1, p. 107).

Any representation of the confederates' meeting is preceded by an acknowledgement of the *Puszcza* surroundings, which gives the rebels and their haunt a tinge of banditti flair. The most memorable of these scenes is when the members of the clandestine organisation are presented. The Polish bandits are conventionally objectified, in a manner reminiscent of gothic landscape with banditti paintings: '—whatever else was wanting in their external presentment, the picturesque was there in all its vigour of wildness', we read (vol. 1, p. 108). At the same time, they are also depicted as immersed in the *Puszcza* surroundings, displaying an inherent affinity with the forest: 'Hewers of wood and drawers of water, Xawery's associates boasted all the marked individuality which characterises those in habitual contact with the woods,—untrammelled by social conventions, and accustomed to look on nature face to face' (vol. 1, p. 108). Their immersion in nature is referred to as both testimony to 'barbarism' and 'a total want of enlightenment', but also a source of their perhaps naive, though attractively prelapsarian, understanding of freedom:

> All that could be learned from superficial nature, they knew. The shadowy forest, the blue sky, the gladsome river, had whispered to them that *they* too had an inheritance in the land, and that it was not by the will of Providence they were scourged into adhesion to this or that allotment of the glebe;—that the Creator,—who has written on the tables of his law a sympathy of brotherhood throughout the human race, and vouchsafed, in the plenitude of his mercy, redemption unto all mankind,—had not ordained the foot of the oppressor to bow down their necks into the dust, nor their children to be born to the bitter bread of bondage.—They knew all this, for they *felt* it;—the sermons written on their forest trees, and the books of their running brooks, had inculcated the lesson. (vol. 1, pp. 110–11)

The *Puszcza*, an uncultivated, centuries-old forest, is thus the seat of natural wisdoms, which complicates the conventional binary of barbarism and civilisation. The rebels feed on the *Puszcza*, and when they eventually march towards the *Ratusz* (City Hall), which Gore compares to the Inquisition (vol. 2, p. 55), each is 'bearing in his hands a beechen bough' (vol. 2, p. 187), in a *Macbeth*-like manner, so that their rustling sounds would both identify them as the people of the *Puszcza* (amongst affiliated revolutionaries) and provoke more fear in their enemies. The implied idea is of the all-encompassing, ungovernable and inherently wild *Puszcza*, embodied by the picturesque and wild rebels, closing in on a decaying feudal order with scythe and fire, as the beacons lit and carried by the confederates create 'a lurid illumination of the clouds' (vol. 2, pp. 224–5), giving the impression of an apocalyptic hellish glow that reflects itself 'on the sallow cheek' of the mayor (vol. 2, p. 230).

The insurrection is brutally quenched, and the eruption of natural freedom contained within its original boundaries. As stated before, Gore's narrative voice only tentatively supports the liberal sentiment. 'Pasieka', as we have seen, warns against cross-class marriage; the uncultivated, but well-meaning, confederates of Lubionki, as they march towards the town, are joined by other confederations, and the revolutionary mass as a whole becomes more a threat than a promise of a brighter future. The invariably chaste and patriotic freedom fighter is highly born Juliusz Felinski, who notices the ungovernable and destructive fervour of the mass, fuelled by drunkenness and the desire for revenge. In the end, Gore does not offer a consistent challenge to Gothic Poland as a land of serfdom and inequalities, and the abolitionist cause is qualified by anti-revolutionary sentiments.

At the same time, a symbolic demolition of the *ancien régime* is indeed brought about in the tale, though not by the *Puszcza* revolutionaries but another 'forest being'. Just like Porter in *Thaddeus*, Gore avails herself of female gothic frameworks to go beyond the historically specific narrative of Poland and to address more general political issues of the imperilled and imprisoned female body. A seemingly secondary character Doska (or Doroska) is abused and deserted by one of the protagonists, the foppish Konstanty Felinski. She roams the *Puszcza*, producing sounds and songs that the other visitors to the forest take to be supernatural. Seriously injured, she is accidentally saved by Konstanty, only to be imprisoned later on by the Jesuits, following the unjust suspicion of murder once her saviour and abuser vanishes. Doska contains within herself several gothic narratives: she is victimised by a vampiric nobleman, taken for the spectral 'Forest Lady', and finally becomes a prisoner of scheming monks. As such, she becomes Gore's instrument in the catastrophic resolution, whereby a major part of the Jesuit establishment and the City Hall are destroyed. Imprisoned in an underground vault, close to the rebels' ammunition store, Doska is convinced of the tragic death of Konstanty in the struggles, and 'in the frenzy of the delusion' casts a torch towards the stocked powder barrels (vol. 2, p. 271). The explosion is a symbolic catastrophe, burying the old rule, although its purifying function is limited. It coincides with the death of King August III and the promises of the new election, combined with a general pardon for all parties involved; but since Gore's is a historical narrative, her readers would have known full well that the reforms of the new king were to be very short lived, that serfdom continued (a project to abolish it in the Russian-controlled Congress Poland was voted against in 1830), and that Poland would eventually be partitioned and enslaved herself. Doska's act of revenge is thus more successful – despite her literal intentions – within the *Jane Eyre*-like female gothic framework. Doska becomes a frenzied instrument of destruction, believing Konstanty is dead, whereas in fact it is the explosion that kills both herself and Konstanty. Just like Bertha Mason fourteen years later, Doska sets on fire both the seat of gender oppression and the abusive relationship with the rake Felinski, which she would not otherwise intentionally relinquish.

Conclusion

The variety of fictional responses to the Polish revolutions between the 1790s and the 1830s collectively form a textual corpus that is confirmatory of several already recognised qualities of British gothic fiction in the period. These range from the more general functions of the gothic as a touchstone for revolutionary thought and activism – whether in the 'classic' form of opposition against political tyranny or in the early attempts at fighting social injustice – to the specific formal choices that characterised these narratives, especially as far as spatial representation, character construction, and emplotment were concerned. The formulaic employment of a set of familiar aesthetic techniques, such as repetition, obfuscation, spatial and temporal ambiguity, and stylistic excess, rather than being a manifestation of poor-quality, derivative writing, should be viewed as realising a specific communicational situation, with recycling seen as conducive to achieving predetermined aesthetic and political effects.

Nevertheless, this Element has shown that in deriving inspiration from the Polish question in the period, British writers were able to go beyond the familiar and to uncover aspects of Gothic Poland that could enrich contemporaneous gothic writing. Newly discovered (in fiction) geographical localities, such as the mines or ancient forests, added a further dimension to the ways in which the gothic made sense of nature, time, and space, whereas the prevalent use of anti-royal conspiracies, clandestine organisations, dispossession and exile, while already known in gothic writing, acquired special currency in the light of the actual political events. The fall of Poland, once a powerful agent on the European political stage, concretised the popular metaphors of ruins and bygone regimes. What happened to Poland provided a re-enactment of the gothic's foundational myth: the sack of Rome by the Goths. While the ruins of the Roman Empire provoked reflections on civilisation and barbarism, the passing of time, and the fall of the ancient state, those reflections would have been cherished and cultivated from a position of distance – temporal and geographical – and without an immediate political relevance. The fall of Poland, in turn, was closer to home, and its effects were not only noticeable from a parliamentary point of view, but also from the perspective of an 'average' press and fiction reader, or a passer-by who came across exiles remindful of Porter's Thaddeus on the streets of London. The conceptual identification of Poland and ancient Rome, which informs the gothic underplot of *Thaddeus of Warsaw* through the fictionalised representation of Villanow, as has been discussed, is also suggested in Clairmont and Shelley's 'The Pole', as Ladislaus reflects upon a Neapolitan vista:

> It would be difficult to define the feelings of the traveller as he gazed on this scene: his countenance, uplifted to heaven, was animated with a profound and impassioned melancholy, with an expression of an earnest and fervid pleading against some vast and inevitable wrong. He was thinking of his country; and whilst he contrasted its ruined villages and devastated fields with the splendour and glow of the fair land before him, was breathing inwardly a passionate appeal against that blind and cruel destiny which had consigned Poland to the desolating influence of Russian despotism.[139]

As the link is established at the very beginning of the story, with Ladislaus first confronted with Italian scenery, the setting of the ensuing intrigue against Ladislaus, including some of the best known ancient edifices of Naples, is endowed with a current political significance, whereby it becomes an illustration of the Pole's melancholic disposition and a stage for further cruelty against the representative of a newly ruined state.

The feminisation of Poland, in turn – and we must recall that the male victims, such as Stanisław August Poniatowski, Tadeusz Kościuszko, Porter's Thaddeus, and Clairmont and Shelley's Ladislaus, are all depicted as combining heroism with effeminacy – allowed for the gothic story of the fall to be endowed with female gothic imagery, again something that the prevalent use of the ruins of ancient Rome did not offer. As we have seen, Poland's suffering body politic, of which the gothic castle – decaying, invaded, or penetrated by enemies – is metonymic, tends to be also identified with the imperilled female body, and the stories of Anzoletta Zadoski, Rhodiska, Therese Sobieski, Axinia, and Doska underline the applicability of female gothic patterns in order to make sense of the broader political situation, and, conversely, to generalise and allegorise 'grand' history so that it could be read as relevant on the personal level.

Gothic Poland provided a unique space for integrating foreignness, at times orientalised, with relevance. While gothic fiction set in more popular contexts, such as the Mediterranean or Germany, combined the displacement agenda with geographical and cultural obfuscation, so that the allure of the exotic setting would not dominate the actual meanings implied, the Polish setting of the analysed corpus at times comes to the fore, and the otherwise prevalent Italianate conventions for spatial representation are balanced with country-specific observations. This drive towards accuracy, however, is not merely aimed at travel or historical writing-type readerly appeal. Recycling materials from such sources as Coxe's *Travels* or

---

[139] Clairmont and Shelley, 'The Pole', pp. 276–7.

Jones's *History*, and the regular press coverage devoted to the Polish question, was yet another method geared towards relevance, with particular instances of political events, historical characters, and actual places absorbed into the gothic universe and creatively transformed with a new audience in mind. The cognitive tension is best visible in Gore's *Polish Tales*. On the one hand, in representing the Polish realities it is the most accurate text of the corpus discussed in this Element, perhaps too accurate in terms of the repetitive uses of the Polish language, which might seem alienating; but, on the other hand, it is grounded in current British affairs, such as the proto-democratic Reform Act of 1832 and abolitionist discourse, as well as responding to the wider atmosphere of revolution and nationalist sentiment in early 1830s Europe.

This Element has asserted that while fiction tended to be ignored in previous attempts at reading British responses to the Polish revolutions of the 1790s and the 1830s, it constituted an extensive and versatile corpus of work with a number of examples that went beyond the allure of novelty and exoticism in order to problematise the Polish cause in the context of what was happening at home. This was a continuing quality of concomitant political discourse, with homely affairs and concerns often perceived as obstacles to any form of the direct involvement of Britain in the struggles and sufferings of 'the country in the moon'; but these fictional responses, freed of the activist imperative, managed to offer a wider-ranging reflection, effectively spanning the imaginative timeframe between the fall of Rome and the modern revolutions of the 1830s.

Bibliography

Adams, John, *A View of Universal History ... Including an Account of the Celebrated Revolutions in France, Poland, Sweden, Geneva* (London: G. Kearsley, 1795).

An Authentic Narrative of Facts Relative to the Late Dismemberment of Poland (London: J. Owen, 1794).

Bayley, Frederic William Naylor, *Tales of the Late Revolutions: With A Few Others* (London: Dalton, 1831).

Belcher, Samantha Lee, '"A most vexatious trade to make bread by": The Authorial Careers of Christian Isobel Johnstone and Catherine Gore, 1824–1846' (PhD diss., Durham University, 2021).

Benyowsky, Mauritius August, Count de, *The Memoirs and Travels of Mauritius August Count de Benyowsky*, 2 vols (London: G. G. J. and J. Robinson, 1788).

Bienstock Anolik, Ruth, *Property and Power in English Gothic Literature* (Jefferson: McFarland, 2016).

Boruwlaski, Joseph, *Memoires du Célèbre Nain Joseph Boruwlaski; Memoirs of the Celebrated Dwarf, Joseph Boruwlaski* (Londres/London, 1788).

Burke, Edmund, *The Speeches of the Right Honourable Edmund Burke in the House of Commons and in Westminster Hall*, 4 vols (London: Longman, Hurst, Rees, Orme and Brown, 1816).

Burke, Edmund, *A Philosophical Enquiry into the Origin of our Ideas of the Sublime and Beautiful*, edited by Adam Phillips (Oxford: Oxford University Press, 1998).

Campbell, Thomas, *The Pleasures of Hope and Other Poems* (Edinburgh: Mundell & Son; and Longman & Rees, and J. Wright, 1795).

Canuel, Mark, *Religion, Toleration and British Writing, 1790–1830* (Cambridge: Cambridge University Press, 2002).

Chaplin, Sue, *The Gothic and the Rule of Law, 1764–1820* (Basingstoke: Palgrave Macmillan, 2007).

Charlton, Mary, *Phedora; or, the Forest of Minski*, 4 vols (London: Minerva, 1798).

Copeland, Edward, *The Silver Fork Novel: Fashionable Fiction in the Age of Reform* (Cambridge: Cambridge University Press, 2012).

Corbett, Marion and Margaret, *Tales and Legends*, 3 vols (Edinburgh: Cadell; London: Simpkin and Marshall, 1828).

Couvray, Jean-Baptiste Louvet de, *The Life and Adventures of the Chevalier de Faublas: Including a Variety of Anecdotes Relative to the Present King of Poland*, 4 vols (London: R. Faudler, 1793).

Coxe, William, *Travels into Poland, Russia, Sweden, and Denmark*, 2 vols (London: T. Cadell, 1784).

Cusack, Andrew and Barry Murnane (eds), *Popular Revenants: The German Gothic and Its International Reception, 1800–2000* (Rochester: Camden House, 2012).

Cybowski, Milosz K., 'The Polish Questions in British Politics and Beyond, 1830–1847' (PhD diss., University of Southampton, 2016).

Cybowski, Milosz K., 'Brave and Patriotic Poles: British Politics and Polish Independence, 1830–1847', in Maggie Ann Bowers and Ben Dew (eds), *Polish Culture in Britain: Literature and History, 1772 to the Present* (Cham: Palgrave Macmillan, 2023), pp. 39–61.

Davies, Norman, *Heart of Europe: The Past in Poland's Present* (Oxford: Oxford University Press, 2001).

DeLisle, Emma, *A Soldier's Offspring; or, The Sisters. A Tale*, 2 vols (London: Minerva, 1810).

DeLucia, JoEllen. 'Radcliffe Incorporated: Ann Radcliffe, Mary Ann Radcliffe and the Minerva Author', *Romantic Textualities: Literature and Print Culture, 1780–1840* 23 (2020): 94–108.

Demata, Massimiliano (ed.), 'Italy and the Gothic', a special issue of *Gothic Studies* 8:1 (2006).

Demetrius, a Russian Romance, 2 vols (London: Longman, 1813).

Dibdin, Charles, 'Explanatory Sketch of the new Serious Pantomime of Blackenberg; or, The Spirit of the Elbe', in *Songs, &c. in the Burletta of the Bird Catcher: Or, Catch as Catch Can. With a Copious Description of the Story of the New Pantomime of Peter Wilkins: or, Harlequin in the Flying World. And Also of the New Splendid Ballet Spectacle of Blackenberg; or, Spirit of the Elbe. As Performed at Sadler's Wells* (London, 1800).

Drozdowski, Piotr J., 'Echoes of the Polish Revolution in Late Eighteenth and Early Nineteenth Century English Literature (A Selection of Works and Voices: Part One)', *The Polish Review* 38:1 (1993): 3–24.

Drozdowski, Piotr J., 'Echoes of the Polish Revolution in Late Eighteenth and Early Nineteenth Century English Literature (A Selection of Works and Voices: Part Two)', *The Polish Review* 38:2 (1993): 131–48.

Garside, Peter, et al., 'The English Novel, 1800–1829 & 1830–1836. Update 8 (April 2000–June 2023)', *Romantic Textualities: Literature and Print Culture, 1780–1840* 24 (2023): 197–305.

Garside, Peter, James Raven, and Rainer Schöwerling, *The English Novel 1770–1829: A Bibliographical Survey of Prose Fiction Published in the British Isles. Volume I, 1770–1799.* Oxford: Oxford University Press, 2000.

Garside, Peter, James Raven, and Rainer Schöwerling, 'The English Novel in the Romantic Era: Consolidation and Dispersal', in Peter Garside, James Raven, and Rainer Schöwerling, *The English Novel, 1770–1829: A Bibliographical Survey of Prose Fiction Published in the British Isles*, 2 vols (Oxford: Oxford University Press, 2000), vol. 2, pp. 15–103.

Gilbert, Sandra M. and Susan Gubar, *The Madwoman in the Attic: The Woman Writer and the Nineteenth-Century Literary Imagination* (New Haven: Yale University Press, 1984).

Gleason, John Howes, *The Genesis of Russophobia in Great Britain: A Study of the Interaction of Policy and Opinion* (Cambridge, MA: Harvard University Press, 1950).

Gołębiowska, Zofia, 'Jane Porter – angielska admiratorka Tadeusza Kościuszki', *Annales Universitatis Mariae Curie-Skłodowska* 56 (2001): 7–15.

Gore, Catherine Frances, *Theresa Marchmont; or, The Maid of Honour. A Tale* (London: J. Andrews, 1824).

Gore, Catherine Frances, *The Lettre de Cachet; A Tale. The Reign of Terror; A Tale* (London: J. Andrews, 1827).

Gore, Catherine Frances, *Polish Tales*, 3 vols (London: Saunders and Otley, 1833).

Gore, Catherine, *Cecil: or, The Adventures of a Coxcomb (1841)*, edited by Andrea Hibbard and Edward Copeland, *Silver Fork Novels, 1826–1841*, vol. 6 (London: Pickering & Chatto, 2005).

Gottlieb, Evan, 'No Place Like Home: From Local to Global (and Back Again) in the Gothic Novel', in Evan Gottlieb and Juliet Sheilds (eds), *Representing Place in British Literature and Culture: From Local to Global, 1660–1830* (Farnham: Ashgate, 2013), pp. 85–101.

Groom, Nick, 'The Term "Gothic" in the Long Eighteenth Century, 1680–1800', in Angela Wright and Dale Townshend (eds), *The Cambridge History of the Gothic. Volume I: Gothic in the Long Eighteenth Century* (Cambridge: Cambridge University Press, 2020), pp. 44–66.

Hales, J. M. H., *De Willenberg; or, The Talisman. A Tale of Mystery*, 4 vols (London: A. K. Newman, 1821).

Hansard, House of Commons, 9 July 1833, vol. 19, https://hansard.parliament.uk/Commons/1833-07-09/debates/53d3c4d4-d814-4625-a74d-d747d4cf9fb6/AffairsOfPoland.

Hogle, Jerrold E., 'Abjection as Gothic and the Gothic as Abjection', in Jerrold E. Hogle and Robert Miles (eds), *The Gothic and Theory: An Edinburgh Companion* (Edinburgh: Edinburgh University Press, 2019), 108–26.

Howell, Ann, *Anzoletta Zadoski: A Novel*, 2 vols (London: Minerva, 1796).

Hudson, Hannah Doherty, *Romantic Fiction and Literary Excess in the Minerva Press Era* (Cambridge: Cambridge University Press, 2023).

Hughes, Winifred, 'Gore [née Moody], Catherine Grace Frances (1798–1861)', *Oxford Dictionary of National Biography Online*, https://doi.org/10.1093/ref:odnb/11091.

Jasiakiewicz, Wojciech, *Brytyjska opinia publiczna wobec powstania listopadowego w okresie 1830-1834* (Toruń: Wydawnictwo Uniwersytetu Mikołaja Kopernika, 1997).

Jones, Stephen, *The History of Poland* (London: Vernor and Hood, 1795).

Kelly, Gary, *English Fiction of the Romantic Period, 1789–1830* (London and New York: Longman, 1989).

Kilgour, Maggie, *The Rise of the Gothic Novel* (London: Routledge, 1995).

Killick, Tim, *British Short Fiction in the Early Nineteenth Century: The Rise of the Tale* (Aldershot: Ashgate, 2008).

Koźmian, Stanisław, *Anglia i Polska* (Poznań: Nakładem Księgarni Jana Konstantego Żupańskiego, 1862).

Lafontaine, August Heinrich Julius, *Dolgorucki and Menzikof. A Russian Tale*, 2 vols (London: Minerva, 1805).

Laskowski, Maciej, 'Jane Porter's *Thaddeus of Warsaw* as Evidence of Polish-British Relationships' (PhD diss., Adam Mickiewicz University, 2012).

Lathom, Francis, *The Polish Bandit; Or, Who is My Bride?, and Other Tales* (London: A. K. Newman, 1824).

Lathy, Thomas Pike, *The Invisible Enemy; or, The Mines of Wielitska. A Polish Legendary Romance*, 4 vols (London: Minerva, 1806).

Lewis, Matthew Gregory, *The Monk*, intr. Stephen King (Oxford: Oxford University Press, 2002).

Lines, Joe, 'William Lane, the Ramble Novel and the Genres of Romantic Irish Fiction', *Romantic Textualities: Literature and Print Culture, 1780–1840* 23 (2020): 21–38.

Lipoński, Wojciech, *Polska a Brytania 1801–1830: Próby politycznego i cywilizacyjnego dźwignięcia kraju w oparciu o Wielką Brytanię* (Poznań: Wydawnictwo Naukowe Uniwersytetu im. Adama Mickiewicza w Poznaniu, 1978).

Lodoiska; or, The Tartar Robber: An Historic Tale (London: J. Roe & Ann Lemoine, 1811).

Looser, Devoney, 'The Great Man and Women's Historical Fiction: Jane Porter and Sir Sidney Smith', *Women's Writing* 19:3 (2012): 293–314.

Looser, Devoney, *Sister Novelists: The Trailblazing Porter Sisters, Who Paved the Way for Austen and the Brontës* (London: Bloomsbury, 2022). Epub ebook.

McAleavey, Maia, *The Bigamy Plot: Sensation and Convention in the Victorian Novel* (Cambridge: Cambridge University Press, 2015).

McLean, Thomas, 'Nobody's Argument: Jane Porter and the Historical Novel', *Journal for Early Modern Cultural Studies* 7:2 (2007): 88–103.

McLean, Thomas, *The Other East and Nineteenth-Century British Literature: Imagining Poland and the Russian Empire* (Basingstoke: Palgrave Macmillan, 2012).

McLean, Thomas, 'Introduction', in Jane Porter, *Thaddeus of Warsaw*, edited by Thomas McLean and Ruth Knezevic (Edinburgh: Edinburgh University Press, 2022), pp. viii–xxiii.

Memorial on the Present State of Poland (London: J. Debrett, 1791).

Milton, John, *Paradise Lost*, intr. Philip Pullman (Oxford: Oxford University Press, 2005).

Minifie, Margaret, *The Count de Poland*, 4 vols (London: J. Dodsley, 1780).

Murray, Mrs., *Henry Count the Kolinski: A Polish Tale* (London: James Cawthorn, 1810).

Neiman, Elizabeth A., *Minerva's Gothics: The Politics and Poetics of Romantic Exchange, 1780–1820* (Cardiff: University of Wales Press, 2019).

Neiman, Elizabeth and Christina Morin (eds), 'The Minerva Press and the Literary Marketplace', a special issue of *Romantic Textualities: Literature and Print Culture, 1780–1840* 23 (2020).

Newton, Michael and Evert Jan van Leeuwen (eds), *Haunted Europe: Continental Connections in English-Language Gothic Writing, Film and New Media* (London and New York: Routledge, 2020).

O'Malley, Patrick R., '"It may be remembered": Spatialized Memory and Gothic History in *The Mysteries of Udolpho*', *The Eighteenth Century* 59:4 (2018): 493–512.

Peiser, Megan, 'William Lane and the Minerva Press in the Review Periodical, 1790–1820', *Romantic Textualities: Literature and Print Culture, 1780–1840* 23 (2020): 124–48.

Peltier, M., *Paris, Pendant L'Année 1798* (Londres: Deboffe, Dulau, Boosey, 1798).

Pigault-Lebrun, Charles-Antoine, *The Polanders; The Lying Family; and The Life of My Uncle, with His Portfolio* (London: Minerva, 1805).

Porter, Jane, *The Spirit of the Elbe*, 2 vols (London: T. N. Longman and O. Rees, 1799).
Porter, Jane, *Thaddeus of Warsaw* (London: T. N. Longman and O. Rees, 1803).
Porter, Jane, *Thaddeus of Warsaw*, rev. ed. (London: Henry Colburn and Richard Bentley, 1831).
Porter, Jane, *Thaddeus of Warsaw*, edited by Thomas McLean and Ruth Knezevic (Edinburgh: Edinburgh University Press, 2022).
Potter, Franz J., *The History of Gothic Publishing, 1800–1835: Exhuming the Trade* (Basingstoke: Palgrave Macmillan, 2005).
Price, Fiona, *Reinventing Liberty: Nation, Commerce and the Historical Novel from Walpole to Scott* (Edinburgh: Edinburgh University Press, 2016).
Punter, David, *The Literature of Terror: A History of Gothic Fictions from 1765 to the Present Day*, 2 vols (Harlow: Longman, 1996).
Pyrhönen, Heta, *Bluebeard Gothic*: Jane Eyre *and Its Progeny* (Toronto: University of Toronto Press, 2010).
[Radcliffe, Mary Anne?], *Radzivil: A Romance*, 3 vols (London: W. Lane, 1790).
Raspe, Rudolph Erich, *Gulliver Revived; or the Singular Travels, Campaigns, Voyages, and Adventures of Baron Munikhouson, Commonly Called Munchausen*, 3rd ed. (Oxford: G. Kearsley, 1786).
Sadoff, Dianne F. 'The Silver Fork Novel', in John Kucich and Jenny Bourne Taylor (eds), *The Oxford History of the Novel in English: Volume 3: The Nineteenth-Century Novel 1820–1880* (Oxford: Oxford University Press, 2011), pp. 106–21.
Saglia, Diego and Ian Haywood (eds), *Spain in British Romanticism, 1800–1840* (Cham: Palgrave Macmillan, 2018).
Samojlik, Tomasz, Anastasia Fedotova, Piotr Daszkiewicz, and Ian D. Rotherham, *Białowieża Primeval Forest: Nature and Culture in the Nineteenth Century* (Cham: Springer, 2020).
Schmidgen, Wolfram, *Eighteenth-Century Fiction and the Law of Property* (Cambridge: Cambridge University Press, 2002).
Selden, Catherine, *Serena: A Novel*, 3 vols (London: Minerva, 1800).
Shapira, Yael, 'Isabella Kelly and the Minerva Gothic Challenge', *Romantic Textualities: Literature and Print Culture, 1780–1840* 23 (2020): 168–84.
Shapira, Yael, 'The Gothic Novel Beyond Radcliffe and Lewis', in Angela Wright and Dale Townshend (eds), *The Cambridge History of the Gothic. Volume I: Gothic in the Long Eighteenth Century* (Cambridge: Cambridge University Press, 2020), pp. 323–344.
Shelley, Mary [and Claire Clairmont], 'The Pole', in Mary Wollstonecraft Shelley, *Tales and Stories* (London: William Paterson, 1891), pp. 274–310.

Showalter, Elaine, *The Female Malady: Women, Madness, and English Culture, 1830-1980* (Harmondsworth: Penguin, 1985).

Summers, Montague, *A Gothic Bibliography* (London: The Fortune Press, 1940).

Summers, Montague, *The Gothic Quest: A History of the Gothic Novel* (London: The Fortune Press, 1968).

Sykes, S., *Sir William Dorien: A Domestic Story*, 3 vols (London: Minerva, 1812).

Townshend, Dale, *Gothic Antiquity: History, Romance, and the Architectural Imagination, 1760-1840* (Oxford: Oxford University Press, 2019).

Townshend, Dale and Angela Wright (eds), *The Cambridge History of the Gothic. Volume II: Gothic in the Nineteenth Century* (Cambridge: Cambridge University Press, 2020).

The Calumet: New Series of the Harbinger of Peace 9:1 (1832).

The Critical Review; or, Annals of Literature 26 (1799); 39 (1803).

The Edinburgh New Philosophical Journal 9 (1830).

The Spectator 246 (1833).

Thelwall, John, *The Daughter of Adoption*, 4 vols (London: R. Phillips, 1801).

Wallace, Diana, *The Woman's Historical Novel British Women Writers, 1900–2000* (Basingstoke: Palgrave Macmillan, 2005).

Wallace, Diana, *Female Gothic Histories: Gender, History and the Gothic* (Cardiff: University of Wales Press, 2013).

Wallace, Diana and Andrew Smith, 'Introduction: Defining the Female Gothic', in Diana Wallace and Andrew Smith (eds), *The Female Gothic: New Directions* (Basingstoke: Palgrave Macmillan, 2009), pp. 1–12.

Watt, James, 'Early British Gothic and the American Revolution', in Angela Wright and Dale Townshend (eds), *The Cambridge History of the Gothic. Volume I: Gothic in the Long Eighteenth Century* (Cambridge: Cambridge University Press, 2020), pp. 243–261.

Weiss, Deborah, *Women and Madness in the Early Romantic Novel: Injured Minds, Ruined Lives* (Manchester: Manchester University Press, 2024).

Wester, Maisha, 'Nineteenth-Century British and American Gothic and the History of Slavery', in Dale Townshend and Angela Wright (eds), *The Cambridge History of the Gothic. Volume II: Gothic in the Nineteenth Century* (Cambridge: Cambridge University Press, 2020), pp. 394–415.

Wolff, Larry, *Inventing Eastern Europe: The Map of Civilization on the Mind of the Enlightenment* (Stanford: Stanford University Press, 1994).

Wright, Angela, *Gothic Fiction: A Reader's Guide to Essential Criticism* (Basingstoke: Palgrave Macmillan, 2007).

Wright, Angela, *Britain, France and the Gothic, 1764–1820: The Import of Terror* (Cambridge: Cambridge University Press, 2013).

Wright, Angela, 'Spain in Gothic Fiction', in Diego Saglia and Ian Haywood (eds), *Spain in British Romanticism, 1800–1840* (Cham: Palgrave Macmillan, 2018), pp. 177–93.

Wright, Angela and Dale Townshend (eds), *The Cambridge History of the Gothic. Volume I: Gothic in the Long Eighteenth Century* (Cambridge: Cambridge University Press, 2020).

Zamoyski Adam, 'From the Moon to Kennington Common: British Perceptions of the Poland and the Poles 1750–1850', in Maggie Ann Bowers and Ben Dew (eds), *Polish Culture in Britain: Literature and History, 1772 to the Present* (Cham: Palgrave Macmillan, 2023), pp. 17–38.

Zapatka, Francis E., 'Kościuszko among the English Romantics', *The Polish Review* 30:3 (1985): 239–53.

Zimmerman, Sarah, *The Romantic Literary Lecture in Britain* (Oxford: Oxford University Press, 2019).

Zschokke, Heinrich, *The Polish Chieftain* (London: Minerva, 1806).

Acknowledgements

This Element is the result of a 'Bekker' fellowship at the University of Sheffield, funded by the Polish National Agency for Academic Exchange (NAWA). Aneta, Tadzio, Benio, and Joszko made it a true family adventure, in the best work–life balance tradition imaginable, and I dedicate this work to them. Neither the fellowship nor this Element would have materialised without the help, expertise, and continuous support of Angela Wright, for which I am more than grateful. I would also like to thank Roslyn Irving, Aneta Lipska, Mary Newbould, and Dale Townshend for their insightful comments and precious feedback at various stages of the writing process. I have benefitted substantially from the constructive and encouraging reports I received from the anonymous readers, to which, I hope, the final shape of this Element does justice.

Cambridge Elements =

The Gothic

Dale Townshend
Manchester Metropolitan University
Dale Townshend is Professor of Gothic Literature in the Manchester Centre for Gothic Studies, Manchester Metropolitan University.

Angela Wright
University of Sheffield
Angela Wright is Professor of Romantic Literature in the School of English at the University of Sheffield and co-director of its Centre for the History of the Gothic.

Advisory Board
Enrique Ajuria Ibarra, *Universidad de las Américas, Puebla, Mexico*
Xavier Aldana Reyes, *Manchester Metropolitan University, UK*
Katarzyna Ancuta, *Chulalongkorn University, Thailand*
Carol Margaret Davison, *University of Windsor, Ontario, Canada*
Rebecca Duncan, *Linnaeus University, Sweden*
Jerrold E. Hogle, *Emeritus, University of Arizona*
Mark Jancovich, *University of East Anglia, UK*
Dawn Keetley, *Lehigh University, USA*
Roger Luckhurst, *Birkbeck College, University of London, UK*
Emma McEvoy, *University of Westminster, UK*
Eric Parisot, *Flinders University, Australia*
Andrew Smith, *University of Sheffield, UK*

About the Series
Seeking to publish short, research-led yet accessible studies of the foundational 'elements' within Gothic Studies as well as showcasing new and emergent lines of scholarly enquiry, this innovative series brings to a range of specialist and non-specialist readers some of the most exciting developments in recent Gothic scholarship.

Cambridge Elements =

The Gothic

Elements in the Series

Gothic Voices: The Vococentric Soundworld of Gothic Writing
Matt Foley

Mary Robinson and the Gothic
Jerrold E. Hogle

Folk Gothic
Dawn Keetley

The Last Man and Gothic Sympathy
Michael Cameron

Democracy and the American Gothic
Michael J. Blouin

Dickens and the Gothic
Andrew Smith

Contemporary Body Horror
Xavier Aldana Reyes

The Music of the Gothic 1789–1820
Emma McEvoy

The Eternal Wanderer: Christian Negotiations in the Gothic Mode
Mary Going

African American Gothic in the Era of Black Lives Matter
Maisha Wester

Biography and the Trade-Gothic Author: The case of Isabella Kelly
Yael Shapira

Gothic Poland and British Fiction, c. 1790–1830
Jakub Lipski

A full series listing is available at: www.cambridge.org/GOTH

For EU product safety concerns, contact us at Calle de José Abascal, 56–1°,
28003 Madrid, Spain or eugpsr@cambridge.org.

www.ingramcontent.com/pod-product-compliance
Ingram Content Group UK Ltd.
Pitfield, Milton Keynes, MK11 3LW, UK
UKHW022141240226
468380UK00018B/411